SO-BXK-408

LEAVING IOWA

The Comedy About Family Vacations

by

TIM CLUE and SPIKE MANTON

Dramatic Publishing
Woodstock, Illinois • England • Australia • New Zealand

*** NOTICE ***

©MMVIII by
TIM CLUE and SPIKE MANTON
Printed in the United States of America
All Rights Reserved
(LEAVING IOWA)

ISBN: 978-1-58342-585-5

IMPORTANT BILLING AND CREDIT REQUIREMENTS

All producers of the play *must* give credit to the authors of the play in all programs distributed in connection with performances of the play and in all instances in which the title of the play appears for purposes of advertising, publicizing or otherwise exploiting the play and/or a production. The names of the authors *must* also appear on a separate line, on which no other name appears, immediately following the title, and *must* appear in size of type not less than fifty percent (50%) the size of the title type. Biographical information on the authors, if included in the playbook, may be used in all programs. *In all programs this notice must appear:*

"Produced by special arrangement with
THE DRAMATIC PUBLISHING COMPANY of Woodstock, Illinois"

In addition, all producers of the play must include the following acknowledgment on the title page of all programs distributed in connection with performances of the play and on all advertising and promotional materials:

"*Leaving Iowa* premiered at the Purple Rose Theatre Company
on January 22, 2004, in Chelsea, Michigan,
directed by Anthony Caselli."

Acknowledgments

Thanks to artistic director Guy Sanville, *Leaving Iowa* premiered at Jeff Daniels' Purple Rose Theatre Company on January 22, 2004, in Chelsea, Mich. It was directed by Anthony Caselli, with John Lepard as Don, Grant Krause as Dad, Elizabeth Ann Townsend as Mom, Teri Clark as Sis and Jim Porterfield as the multiple character guy. We will always be grateful for the opportunity the Purple Rose extended to us.

A special thanks to Shawn Pace our production manager for his extraordinary work and guidance throughout the process.

LEAVING IOWA

For an ensemble cast of six actors

<u>CHARACTERS</u>

DON BROWNING . . adult writer, young boy in flashbacks

DAD . . . . Don's dad

MOM . . . . Don's mom, past and present

SIS . . . . Don's sister, past and present

MULTIPLE CHARACTER GUY - in order of appearance

FARMER JOHNSON . . . . farmer with silo
GRANDPA . . . . Don's grandfather
CART GUY . . . . grocery store employee
UNCLE PHIL . . . . Don's uncle
JOE HOFINGERS . . . . farmer with hoe
AMISH GUY . . . . Amish peddler at flea market
CIVIL WAR GUY . . . . Civil War performer/narrator
JACK SINGER . . . . Don's childhood friend, now professor
MECHANIC . . . . fixes Don's car
PARK RANGER . . . . park ranger
CLERK . . . . unhappy old man
WAYNE . . . . stoic waiter with mullet
BOB . . . . hog farmer

5

MULTIPLE CHARACTER GAL - in order of appearance

MRS. JOHNSON . . . . farmer wife with silo
GRANDMA . . . . Don's grandmother
AUNT PHYLLIS. . . . . Don's aunt
AMISH GAL . . . . Amish peddler at flea market
MUSEUM ASSISTANT . . . . . Civil War Guy's announcer
JAMIE. . . . . mechanic
DRUNK LADY . . . . patron in hotel
JESSIE. . . . . talkative waitress
JUDY . . . . hog farmer Bob's wife

See Production Notes, Set Notes, Sound Design CD Notes
and Prop List at end of play..

ACT I

(SFX: Music: "I've Been Iowhere" used before the show begins. SFX: Pre-show announcement and song: "1000 Miles to the Middle of Everywhere." SFX: Driving music opens play to DAD driving.

Lights up—a family driving at night. DON and SIS are sleeping in the back seat and MOM is sleeping in the front seat. DAD is driving, tired, doing all the things one might do to stay awake, but his head nods into his chest once, pops back up, and then again and pops back. On the third head nod his head stays down, fully asleep. After a beat: SFX: Loud truck horn blast. DAD's head snaps up as the family is startled awake.)

DAD & FAMILY. AHHHHHHHHHHHHHHHHHHH!

(Everyone is disoriented.)

MOM. Oh goodness, honey, what was that?
DAD. Nothing, nothing. Just some truck out of control. Probably nodding off at the wheel.
SIS. Mom?
DAD. Go back to sleep, sweetpea.
DON. Dad?

DAD. Close your eyes, big guy. Back to sleep, everyone. *(To MOM.)* Just some trucker nodding off a bit.

MOM. What was it?

DAD. Just some crazy sleepy trucker, close your eyes, honey.

MOM. Oh my goodness, how long have I been out?

DAD. Not long, sweetheart. We're OK. Just close your eyes...and go back to sleep.

MOM. Where are we?

DAD. Almost there. Close your—

MOM. Honey, where are we?

SIS. Dad, where are we?

MOM. Shouldn't we be home by now? *(Pause.)* Honey, are we—

DAD. No, we are not lost.

DON. Dad?

DAD. Close your eyes, big guy.

MOM. What road is this?

DON. What's going on?

SIS. I think he's lost.

DAD. Close your eyes, sweetie.

SIS. What time is it?

MOM. It's 3:30.

MOM, DON & SIS. 3:30!

MOM. Honey...

DAD. Little mix-up.

SIS. Dad!

MOM. Do we have a mile marker?

DAD. No.

MOM. So we are lost.

DAD. No, we are not.

MOM. Then why aren't we home?

DAD. A little out of our way maybe, *(MOM is looking for mile markers)* but not lost. We're getting there.

SIS. Getting where?

DAD. Calm down, honey.

SIS. Where are we getting? *(Beat.)* Where are we? *(Beat.)* Why isn't anyone answering me?

DAD. Because it's time to go to sleep. Everyone back to sleep.

MOM. Help me look for a mile marker.

DON. I'm thirsty.

MOM. In a minute, Don.

(SIS punches DON in shoulder. Together they hunch around DAD.)

DON.	SIS.
Dad!	Dad!

DAD. I said back to sleep.

MOM. Is everybody looking? A mile marker would really help.

(Now they hunch over MOM.)

SIS.	DON.
Mom?	Mom?

MOM. Everyone, I'm looking for a mile marker. We need a mile marker. Can we all just look for a mile marker?!

DAD *(snatches map from MOM)*. Here, let's take a look.

MOM. Honey, not while you're driving.

DAD.	MOM.
I got it, got it. I got it.	Sweetheart?

(DAD focused on the map, veers into other lane. SFX: Loud honk.)

MOM.	DON & SIS.
HONEY, look out!	DAAAAAD!

MOM *(snatches map back)*. Give me that! What in heaven's name are you thinking!? *(Smacks DAD with map.)*

DAD. I think I've got it now.

MOM *(beginning to fray)*. Honey, we need a mile marker; kids, we need a mile marker; can we all just look for a mile marker!?

SIS. Mom, this is not fair. This is not fair.

DAD. Let's all settle down.

SIS. Mom, it's not fair, it's not fair. *(Stuttering.)* It's it's it's it's it's like we're hostages…

DAD. Stop it or I will pull over. I swear I will.

(While SIS continues, MOM, DAD and DON repeat their lines in a crescendo of chaos until DAD announces that he is pulling over.)

SIS. Why do we need a family vote if the promise isn't going to matter?

DAD. Who's not sleeping?

SIS. Why do we vote if it's not going to matter?

MOM.	DAD.
Honey, not now!	Who's not sleeping!

DON. Mo-o-om—

MOM. Looking for a mile marker... *(Repeat and build with others.)*

SIS. If it's not going to matter then why do we vote? Right, Mom!?

DON. Mo-o-o-om—

MOM. Need a mile marker.

DAD. I'm warning you!

SIS. Right, Mom?

DON. Mo-o-o-o-o-o-o-o-om—

DAD. I'm warning you. *(Barely controlled.)* I am warning you.

SIS *(adamantly)*.	DON.
Well, if it's a vote and a promise, then I promise I am never voting again!	Mo-o-o-o-o-o-o-o-o-o-om!

DAD *(at the end of his rope)*. OK, that's it, that is it! That's it! That is it! I am pulling over!

(SFX: Car on gravel. DAD pulls over. KIDS heads snap up and they retreat quickly to the back seat. There is a long silence while DAD collects himself.)

MOM. We still need a mile marker.

DAD. Everyone, we are not lost. We've uuhhh, just gotten a little off track.

SIS. Mom?

DON.   MOM.
Shh!   Shh!

MOM *(to DAD with great concern)*. Honey?
DAD. OK, OK, OK, look. *(Takes off his glasses.)* Here's
the deal.

(SFX: Car passes. Special on DON. The FAMILY transitions off.)

DON *(almost in one breath)*. Here's the deal. About forty-six hours ago I flew in from Boston to return to my hometown of Winterset, Iowa, and ended up at a hog farm somewhere not too far from Lebanon, Kansas. Which is interesting...

(SFX: Car pass.)

DON *cont'd)*. ...because I had only planned a short drive up and over to my father's childhood home in Mount Union, Iowa, but if that were the case I probably would have never pulled over a few hours away from home in an attempt to try and write this story down. A story I promised my mom I would never tell anyone, which is something you shouldn't do if you write a newspaper column, because you almost always end up doing the opposite. But because this trip ended up being the kind of trip you can't ever plan, and because I think of it as more of an adventure than a story...I felt compelled to get it down. I mean adventures in Iowa are like steep hills—hard to come by. So here's the deal.

(SFX: Boxes drop loudly offstage. DON is startled. Lights change. He heads over.)

DON *(cont'd)*. Mom, are you OK?

MOM *(offstage)*. Donald, we don't have time for this.

DON. Mom, I can come down to help you look for it.

OLDER SIS *(offstage)*. I wouldn't if I were you, big brother.

MOM *(offstage)*. We don't have time for this, Don. Not today.

(OLDER SIS enters from the basement.)

OLDER SIS. Don, we can't find it and I'm not happy about this! Not happy!

DON. Sorry, Sis, three years.

OLDER SIS. I know how long it's been, Don, and don't talk to me like that. I begged you not to do this, and especially not today.

(MOM enters flustered and dusty, also from basement.)

MOM. Donald, I give up, I give up, I give up. I can't find it.

DON. Mom, you looked everywhere?

MOM. I've looked everywhere I've looked, young man. *(Flustered.)* Donald, we don't have time for this, we have company coming tonight and you need to relax!

DON. I am relaxed.

MOM. Then why so busy, busy, busy? We thought you were coming home for Joey's baptism, for your sister, and for the dinner tonight, but not for this.

DON. Mom, I came home for all of it.

(OLDER SIS exits back to the basement, upset.)

OLDER SIS. This feels like very poor timing, big brother, very poor timing.
DON. Can I help?
OLDER SIS. I don't need your help, big brother!
DON. Mom? *(MOM starts to cry from the anxiety.)* Mom, I'm sorry, but…

(DON attempts to comfort his MOM but is rebuffed while OLDER SIS is shouting as she bangs boxes around looking.)

OLDER SIS *(offstage)*. Don, just because you live in a big city and write for a big newspaper does not give you the right to walk in here and turn the day upside down… This does not feel right…

(OLDER SIS enters with an urn inside a shabby box.)

OLDER SIS *(cont'd)*. Not today. This was supposed to be our time together—family time—Joey's time. Not this. Not now. *(Now center, she pulls the urn out of the box and blows the dust off. Let the moment settle.)*
MOM. You found him. *(Pause.)*
DON *(stays focused on the urn)*. My father had passed away three years ago, and instead of honoring a rather simple request to be returned to his childhood home…
MOM. Where was he?
OLDER SIS. On top of the fuse box.

DON. We left him in the basement. Three years.

MOM. Three years?

OLDER SIS. Hard to believe.

MOM. Three years.

OLDER SIS. Hard to believe.

MOM. This is all my fault.

OLDER SIS. Mom, it's not your fault.

MOM. I just left him down there.

DON.	OLDER SIS.
Mom, we all did.	Yeah, Mom, I did it, too.

MOM. For three years! No this is my fault. I could be arrested for something like this.

OLDER SIS & DON. Mom, you cannot be arrested.

MOM. Well then humiliated, which is worse. *(Beat.)* Why he wanted to be in this thing in that way I'll never know. *(Upset, near tears.)*

OLDER SIS & DON. It was cheaper. *(They start to laugh.)*

MOM. Oh for heaven's sake.

OLDER SIS. OK, OK, OK then, let's just do this, can we? *(Starts to head out the door.)*

DON. Whoa whoa whoa, where are you going with that?

OLDER SIS. Well I thought we could…

DON. No no no, we can't just go out back and scatter him around the tree.

OLDER MOM. Oh, for heaven's sake.

DON. I'm sorry, Mom, but we all know that Dad wanted to be taken back to Grandma and Grandpa's.

OLDER SIS. But, Donald, Mount Union is two hours from here.

DON. Plenty of time to get back to dinner.

OLDER SIS. Do we even know who lives there now?

DON. Mom?

MOM. I don't think so.

OLDER SIS. So, what, Don, what are you going to do, knock on the door of some stranger and say, excuse me, I'm here to fertilize the lawn?

DON.	MOM.
Oh, that's nice.	Oh, for heaven's sake!

OLDER SIS. I mean really, how long has it been since anyone's even been up there?

MOM. Well, let me think. OK, your father and I took a drive up that way after Grandma passed on...I don't know, maybe nine-ten years ago—and they had painted that beautiful old white house...

DON & OLDER SIS.	MOM.
yellow—why, I'll never know.	yellow—why, I'll never know.

MOM. OK, now stop it. Look, I should do this. I'm the one who left him down there. *(Continues under following crescendo.)*

DON. No, Mom, you have company coming.

OLDER SIS. Look, I'll get a babysitter.

DON. No no no, please.

OLDER SIS. Don, don't fight me on this. Mom has company coming and you have an early flight tomorrow.

DON. Stop, please, please, stop! *(All quiet.)* Now, none of us are any good at saying what we feel. After all, we're from Iowa. *(Beat.)* But you both know why I should do this. OK?

(OLDER SIS hands urn to MOM who hands it to DON.)

MOM. OK, I'll get the keys.

DON. Now that's the Browning spirit.

MOM. And something for you to snack on.

DON. I'm fine.

OLDER SIS. If you are late for dinner...

DON. I promise, I won't be late.

MOM. I'll get you a jacket.

DON. I'm fine.

MOM. And a Krispie treat.

DON *(calling after)*. Mom!

MOM. You'll need a snack on the way up... *(Offstage.)* Don't tell me what I already know...

DON. She can't be stopped. She's an unstoppable helping machine. *(DON stops.)* Hey. *(Takes out a notepad and scribbles. Under breath.)* Unstoppable helping machine.

OLDER SIS. Give it a break, Don. It's called a vacation.

DON. I'm a writer. That's what I do. You're an irritator. That's what you do.

OLDER SIS. Funny, you're funny. Well, OK, just in case you run out of funny things to write about...

DON. What?

OLDER SIS *(hands him an arrowhead)*. I found it while I was digging around down there, thought you might want it.

DON. My arrowhead!

OLDER SIS. But I'll need it back.

DON. You thief! You thief! I knew it! Which trip was this?

OLDER SIS. The last one.

DON. That's right.

OLDER SIS. Yep, one week a year.

DON. That's right. Where was that?

OLDER SIS. Hell.

DON. That's right. That's right.

(MOM enters with stuff.)

MOM. Now, here's a jacket, some Krispie treats and I found an old traveling hat and, oh, and look what else I found. *(Pause.)* One of your father's old traveler guides in case you get lost.

DON. Mom, this thing's a hundred years old.

MOM. Your father would want you to have it.

DON. Well, OK then.

(DON drops map on the seat next to him. MOM retrieves the steering wheel and hands it to DON.)

MOM. Oh, now remember, if it rains you gotta pump it— one, two, three and off. It's been acting up lately. So it's one, two, three and—

OLDER SIS. And off! He's got it, Mom, he's got it.

MOM. You'll call when you get there?

DON. I'll call.

OLDER SIS. He'll call.

DON. You're a thief.

OLDER SIS. Get going.

(As MOM walks away, DON hands OLDER SIS back the coat and Krispie treats. OLDER SIS follows MOM.)

MOM. Now, remember it's one, two, three…one, two, three and…

OLDER SIS. Mom, Mom! He's got it… *(To DON.)* Now don't be late.

DON. I promise.

MOM. Oh goodness, I hope it doesn't rain. *(Calling to DON.)* One, two, three and off!

DON *(shouting while backing out)*. I got it, Mom! I got it! I promise…

OLDER SIS. If he's late for dinner…

(SFX: Car start. DON is backing out while MOM and OLDER SIS talk their way offstage.)

MOM. Oh, did I tell you? Uncle Phil's coming tonight.

OLDER SIS. Uncle Phil? Mom—

MOM. Now, be nice. He's had the gout something awful, be nice.

OLDER SIS. If he's late for dinner, I swear I'll kill him.

MOM. Be nice… I hope it doesn't rain.

OLDER SIS. I swear I'll kill him.

(SFX: DON's driving music. Lights change. DON is driving, adjusts the mirror, stretches, tries on his old cap. He glances at the urn, picks up the traveler's guide and as he is obviously thinking of his father, DAD enters and strolls into the car, leaning against the back seat.)

DON. So whattya think? Can't complain about a day like today, no sir-ree. No sir-ree, picture perfect. *(Pause.)* I guess anything is better than the fuse box. Sorry about that.

(SFX: Car pass.)

DON *(cont'd)*. OK, new band shell in the park—looking good...whoa, new stoplights, very nice. *(Turning.)* Little League park is still looking good. *(Points.)* Right there, ka-bang, first home run. Yep. Remember that? *(Pause.)* Right there, left field, ka-bang, my last home run. Right there. *(Pause.)* If I had known that was it, my only one, I would have run a little slower, kicked up some dirt, waved to a fan—something—but who knew? *(Pause.)* Hey, I hope you don't mind me talking like this...it's just that we've got about 120 miles to go here and it, well, feels like that kind of trip where you need to do some talking. *(Long pause.)* Yeah, well I'm uncomfortable too.

(DON picks up traveler's guide off the seat and looks it over. DAD pops off the back seat as SIS explodes in.)

DAD *(shouting to MOM, offstage)*. Honey! Where's the traveler's guide? Honey? The traveler's guide?
MOM *(offstage)*. Looking for it, can't find it!
SIS *(looking through View-Master)*. Dad, Dad! You gotta look at these! They're all pictures of Iowa. You gotta look at 'em.

(MOM enters with dishtowel. SIS runs to her.)

MOM. Gotta? Sweetheart? Gotta?
SIS. Mom, Mom, Mom, where's the Little Brown Church in the Vale?
MOM. Not right now, sweetie. *(Exits.)*

DAD *(shouting offstage)*. Honey? The traveler's guide?

SIS *(runs to DAD)*. Dad, Dad, Dad, the Herbert Hoover Museum?—is that where they make the vacuums? Dad, you have to look at these!

DAD. Honey, where's the traveler's—

(DON drops the guide back down on the seat.)

DAD *(cont'd)*. Never mind, here it is. Never mind, I found it.

(DAD picks up guide and moves back. SIS stands next to DON, talking to him as if he's there.)

SIS. Oh, Don, wait 'til you see this one. It's so cool, Don! It's got buildings and lights and busy people going everywhere. Look, Don, look! *(Gives up.)* Fine. *(Goes to opposite side of stage, sits quietly and looks through View-Master.)*

DON. Look, I really did come home for the baptism but now everyone thinks I'm trying to jam too much into one day here. *(Pause.)* Hey, Joey's a good kid. Still a little weak on the eye contact and the firm handshake, but he's six months old so there's time. *(Beat.)* Hey, I don't expect Mom and Sis to understand, but this just had to get done, it had to get done, and I think you of all people would cut me a little slack. Needless to say, I think we know who the original busy person was.

(SFX: Car pass.)

DON *(cont'd)*. Hey, was that…? I think it was, the Johnson silo? Yeah, that was it! HA HA! There it was, Dad. My first good look at life outside of Winterset.

(FARMER JOHNSON and MRS. JOHNSON enter.)

MRS. JOHNSON *(agitated)*. What was he thinking? What was he thinking? I mean it. What was he thinking?

FARMER JOHNSON. Now calm down, calm down.

MRS. JOHNSON. Don't tell me to calm down. Tell me what he was thinking. *(Calling up.)* I'm calling your mother, young man! I'm calling his mother.

FARMER JOHNSON. Now don't do that. His father's on the way over.

MRS. JOHNSON. Don't tell me what to do. Because I'm calling her. *(To DON.)* I'm calling your mother! *(Exiting.)* What in the heck was he thinking? *(Exits with FARMER JOHNSON trailing after her.)*

FARMER JOHNSON. Just hold on hold on, now hold on.

(DAD enters scene from back seat.)

DAD. Son! What in the heck were you thinking? What part of that head of yours thought climbing up the Johnson silo was a good idea? I mean, really, just what in the heck were you thinking?

DON *(remembering, smiling)*. I didn't know how to tell you that I climbed all the way up that silo just to look for civilization, maybe a few busy people. But instead all I saw were just a couple more silos.

DAD. Now, I'm not telling your mother because, well, the thought of you up that high might just kill her. So not a word, and I'm not kidding.

DON. I knew you wouldn't understand, because you lived your life by the kind of rules you find shellacked on a block of wood hanging on a string in somebody's kitchen.

(FARMER JOHNSON enters.)

FARMER JOHNSON *(reassuring him)*. That's OK, that's OK, that's OK.

DAD. I'm sure sorry about this, Mel.

FARMER JOHNSON. Oh, that's OK, that's OK, a boy's gotta climb, boy's gotta climb.

DAD. I don't know what in the heck he was thinking.

FARMER JOHNSON. I'm just glad he's safe. Just glad he's safe.

(DAD motions to DON to come over to apologize.)

DON. Sorry, Mr. Johnson, I have no idea what I was thinking. *(Shakes FARMER JOHNSON's hand lamely with head down. DAD moves DON to side. DON wanders a few steps farther away.)*

FARMER JOHNSON. That's OK, son, just glad you're safe. I bet you saw a couple of counties up that far. A couple counties, yes sir. I don't think I ever been up that far.

DAD. Thanks again, Mel. *(Shakes FARMER JOHNSON's hand firmly.)*

FARMER JOHNSON. Oh, that's OK. That's OK. *(Exits.)*

DAD. SON! *(DON is startled.)* Come here! Right here. *(Very firm.)* Son, when you shake a man's hand, you look him in the eye directly. You got that? Especially a man that may have saved your life. You got that? A man's handshake is a tool. Use it correctly and it will bring you friends. OK?

DON. OK.

DAD *(holds out hand. DON shakes with good eye contact. DAD softens)*. OK, that's more like it.

(SFX: Car pass. SIS enters, sits down and plays with the View-Master.)

SIS. Don, c'mere, look at these, they are so cool.

(DAD and DON join the scene with SIS.)

DAD. Now listen up, kids. Time to plan this year's Browning family vacation. *(KIDS react with disappointment.)* Now now now, I know last year you were a little disappointed with our log cabin tour of the Ozarks, so your mother and I are going to try and make it up to you. I've got an idea of my own, but I want to decide this as a family so I'd like to hear some of your ideas. *(Pause. DON and SIS look at each other.)* Really, go ahead.

SIS. Carol's mom and dad went to Las Vegas last year. Carol's mom sprained her ankle, won a hundred dollars and got her purse stolen, but they said it was fun.

DAD. OK, Las Vegas.

DON. How 'bout the Dells?

DAD. No.

DON. Why not?

DAD. Son, that place is nothing but a bunch of fancy, over-priced shenanigans. It's predictable, OK? It's predictable and Brownings are not— *(Pauses and the KIDS say it with him.)*

DAD, SIS, DON. predictable.

DAD *(calling to MOM)*. Any suggestions, dear?

MOM *(still off)*. Not this year.

DON *(calling to MOM)*. How about the Dells?

DAD. No.

MOM *(still off)*. That sounds fun.

(DON looks at DAD.)

DAD. No.

SIS. Dad, Yellowstone.

DAD. Yellowstone?

SIS. Yeah, Jenny Sander's uncle got attacked by a bear and he had to play dead so the bear wouldn't eat him, but they got a really neat picture of it.

DAD. Yellowstone, Las Vegas, OK. Well, those are some good suggestions, but given this year's budget, we need to pull back a bit, but I think I've found a place that's not too far away and should be a lot of fun and looks fascinating. So, who wants to go to…Hannibal, Missouri. Come here, kids.

(KIDS follow DAD and look at the map he is opening up on the table [back seat of the car].)

SIS. Hannibal?

DON. Missouri?

DAD. Yep, so what do you say we vote on it?

SIS. Is there a pool?

DAD. Yep.

DON. Is it near the Dells?

DAD. No.

SIS. But there's a pool?

DAD. You bet there is. And you know what else, sweet-pea? *(Pause.)* It's the home of one of our greatest literary heroes, Mark Twain. All right, let's put this to a family vote.

DON. The family vote.

DAD. Everybody ready? *(To MOM.)* We're voting, honey.

MOM *(still off).* In a minute.

DON. Elections in Cuba were more unpredictable.

SIS. Can't we just go to Grandma and Grandpa's?

DON. I vote for that!

(Both KIDS raise their hands.)

DAD. OK, two votes for Grandma's… Democracy in action…you already know my vote. Two to one. *(Calling to MOM.)* Honey?

(MOM enters.)

MOM. Coming, coming, coming, coming!

DAD. How does Hannibal, Missouri, sound?

MOM. That sounds nice.

DAD. Well, sorry, kids, tie goes to you know who.

DON. Castro.

DAD. Hannibal, Missouri. *(KIDS drop their heads.)* Oh, oh, wait, I've got something for you two! Where did I put those? *(DAD exits. The KIDS slump in exaggerated disappointment.)*

DON. Hannibal.

SIS. Missouri.

MOM. So we're all set?

SIS *(in a hushed tone)*. Mom, I don't wanna go.

MOM. Wanna? Sweetheart, wanna?

SIS. I don't wanna go. I don't—

MOM. Wanna?

SIS *(over-articulating)*. I don't want to go!

MOM. Oh, sweetheart.

SIS. Why can't you, I don't know, drop me off at Grandma's?

MOM. Because we're not.

SIS. But I wanna go—want to go—to Linda Abbalow's party—

MOM. Now listen. Your father has this all planned—

SIS. But, Mom.

MOM. Be a good girl for me?

SIS. Mom—

MOM. Just do this for me, OK?

SIS. But but but but—

(MOM attempts to pull SIS up, but she responds with a combination of spaghetti arms and legs.)

MOM *(sternly)*. Young lady! You know your father looks forward to this trip. He teaches almost all year 'round, this is the one week, the one week a year we take off to do this kind of thing, so the least we can do is help him have a little fun.

SIS. But—

MOM *(now very angry)*. Look! *(Spaghetti arms stop.)* You are going to do this for me and for your father and it is going to be fun. Do you hear me? You will have a LOT OF FUN! And the fun starts NOW!

(DAD reenters with books and tosses one to DON and presents the other to his daughter.)

DAD. Check this out, big guy. And here ya go, sweetpea.

MOM. So, what do you have there, mister?

DON. Short stories.

DAD. By the master himself.

SIS. Thanks, Dad.

DON. Yeah, thanks.

DAD. Look, kids, I promise we'll try and get back to go see Grandma and Grandpa, too, OK?

SIS. OK.

(SFX: Hannibal music.)

DAD. And hey, c'mon now, I promise, kids, this year we're going to have fun.

MOM. And when does the fun start?

DAD. That's right, the fun starts now...and hey, kids, we'll even read some of those stories on the way to Hannibal, huh? Now whattya think of that?

DON & SIS *(resigned)*. OK.

DAD. I'm telling you, kids, Hannibal is going to be fun.

DON. Our vacations were never fun.

DAD. I promise, it's going to be fascinating.

DON. And fascinating was the family vacation f-word.

(FAMILY follows DAD over.)

DAD. C'mere, let's take a look.

(FAMILY is frozen looking at map as DON settles in behind the steering wheel.)

DON. Now, Dad, understand I'm not mad as much as I am amazed. Amazed that every year you managed to find places less interesting than Winterset, Iowa. Do you realize how difficult that is to do?! OK, I admit it, I'm a little upset here, which also makes me a little pathetic, because I'm ranting at a can of ashes, and I should have let this go a long time ago, but really…why not the Dells?
DAD. No.

(DON and DAD exchange positions with a steering-wheel handoff.)

DON. But, Dad, why not?
SIS. Yeah, Dad, why not?
DAD. We don't have time.
DON. But just one day!
SIS. Dad, just one day!
DAD. I told you it's shenanigans, son. Over-priced shenanigans.
DON & SIS. But, Dad!
MOM. Enough! Now we have quite the trip ahead of us here…and I might have some treats for a couple of good quiet kids back there.
SIS *(whispers)*. I can be really really quiet, but I don't think Don can.

DON *(whispers)*. I can be so way much more quiet than
   you.

SIS. You better be quiet or else…

DON. Or else what?

SIS. Or else I'll…

MOM *(finger in air)*. Eh, eh, eh, eh, what part of quiet do
   we not understand?

(The KIDS resettle. SFX: Car pass.)

DAD. OK, mark down the time, honey. It's official, kids,
   we are leaving Winterset. *(Checking odometer.)* Honey,
   it looks like we have 34,322 miles and four-tenths, eh,
   five-tenths. *(DAD does a Bad John Wayne impression
   for the next couple lines.)* Wave goodbye, kids. It's been
   nice knowing you, partner.

MOM *(laughing)*. That was a good one, honey. *(To KIDS.)*
   Do you know who that was?

(The KIDS stare at each other.)

DAD. John Wayne, for goodness sake. Our town is…?
   Home of the Duke. Now you know that. Let me hear
   you say that one, gang. Home of the Duke.

DON & SIS *(lackluster)*. Home of the Duke.

MOM. Oh, he's got it down. Gets me every time…every
   time.

DAD. C'mon, one more time.

DON & SIS *(forced)*. Home of the Duke.

MOM.   DAD.
OK, now that was better.   Not too bad. Home of the
                                  Duke.

*(DON leaves the car on one side as SIS leaves the car
on the other side. MOM and DAD stay in the car, slowly
grabbing books and leaning back as if in bed.)*

DON. Home of the Duke. Boy am I a schmuck. I could've
been there but what'd I do? I call up Sis and ask her to
read for me at your retirement party. I hope you know I
meant it...what was it, something about Winterset being
far more than...

(SIS starts reading from DON's letter.)

SIS. Winterset is more than Home of the Duke. And instead of paying homage to the people who left and never
came back, tonight we pay tribute to a man who stayed,
taught history, coached baseball and changed lives for
forty years.

(SFX: Phone rings. MOM and DAD stay in the car/bed.)

MOM. Oh it was very nice. Mr. Garret says "hi" and
wished you could have been there too, but that's OK, we
know, busy busy busy. But your sister did a nice job.
We were in the back and could hear every word. There
was a bad cougher, sounded like the croup to me, but
she kept right on going. Here, your father wants to talk
to you. *(Whispers.)* Just say hi, just say hi.

DAD. He doesn't want to talk to me. He's too busy— Hey there, big guy. What's the weather like out there?

DON. Congratulations, Dad, I know they're going to miss you.

DAD. Yeah, that's what they say. *(Pause.)* Mr. Garret says "hi."

DON. Yeah, that's what Mom said.

DAD. Boy, the Cougars lost a close one today.

DON. Yeah?

DAD. Yeah, they sure did, a real close one. Still a little weak in the pitching, but we're going on to sectionals… *(Pause.)*

DON. Yeah, well, I bet you're pretty beat.

DAD. Yeah, pretty beat is right.

DON. Yeah. *(Pause.)*

DAD. Oh yeah.

DON. I should have told you that I was proud, that I missed you, and I should have been there. But…

DAD. Yeah, your mother's still up, but I'm pretty beat.

DON *(pause)*. Well, I should let you go then.

DAD. Yep, pretty beat, thanks for calling, son. Hey, son, your sister did a real nice job today, a real nice job… OK, I'll give you back to your mother here.

DON. I should have been there.

(SFX: Car pass. DON and SIS rejoin the car.)

DON & SIS. Mom? Mom? Mom? Mom? Mom?

MOM. OK, OK, OK, well, it sounds like I have two pretty good kids back there who deserve a treat.

(KIDS react and grab treat. A small skirmish erupts that DAD settles. SFX: Car pass.)

DAD. All right now, pay attention, look there, kids...leaving Prairie, population 1,348. Boy, it just keeps growing. So who can tell me what town's next?

SIS. Dad, you ask that every time.

DAD. Oh really? Well then, who wants a nickel?

SIS.	DON.
Pella! Pella! Pella!	Pella! Pella! Pella!
(Grabs nickel.)	

DAD. That's it, sweetpea.

DON. But, Dad, I said it, too.

MOM. Well, that was close.

DON. Dad—

DAD. Maybe next time, big guy. Maybe next time.

(DON and SIS sit back down. DON is feeling cheated.)

SIS. Don, you want to see it? *(SIS holds out the nickel in front of DON, taunting him, then quickly pulls it back.)* Get your own!

DON. Mom!

MOM. Donald, settle down.

DON. But Mom, but Mom, she's doing the pull-back-the-nickel thing and it's not fair!

MOM. Donald!

SIS. But Mom...

MOM. I don't want to hear it! Now take these books and do a little reading...and I mean it.

DON & SIS. But Mom!

DAD. Do what your mother says.

(They take the books and begin to read. After a short pause SIS holds the nickel very close to DON's face taunting but not touching.)

DON. MO-O-O-O-OM!

MOM. Donald!?

DON. But she did the put-the-nickel-close-to-my-face and all and it's really annoying and it's not fair.

SIS. Mom, he said he wanted to see it and I was just showing it to him.

DAD & MOM. All right, enough! *(Pause and drive a bit.)*

DAD *(cont'd)*. Yep, Prairie, Iowa. Hey, did you know, kids, that the first official potato digger was manufactured right back there in Prairie, Iowa? *(Pause.)* Potato digger, first one, Prairie, Iowa. Not a lot people know that. *(Drives for a bit. Pause.)* Ya know, a lot of people think a potato is a root but actually they are specialized underground storage stems, and those stems are called…anyone? "Tubers." Let me hear ya say that one, team. "Tubers."

SIS & DON *(low energy)*. Tubers.

DAD. Now, that was pathetic. Let's try that again… Potatoes are not roots, potatoes are…?

DON & SIS *(forced)*. Tubers.

DAD. That's right! Tubers! Now that's the Browning spirit.

(SFX: Car pass.)

DAD *(excited)*. Hey, everyone, up front, quick, quick. *(KIDS jump up from back seat to lean in the front seat, looking out the front window.)* Now take a look at that! Check this out! *(Pause.)* Alaska license plates. Huh! Now that's a traveler. That's a real traveler. Can you imagine how far they must have… *(Trailing.)* Hmm, I wonder…maybe straight down, maybe across… *(KIDS look at each other and return to the back seat. DAD drives a couple beats.)* So does anyone want to take a guess when we purchased Alaska and for how much? Anyone?

(KIDS quickly open their books to avoid answering.)

MOM. Honey, they're reading.
DAD. Just trying to help.

(They drive a couple beats in silence and then SIS takes her book and smacks her brother on the head, hard.)

DON. MO-O-O-O-OM!

(The KIDS explode, standing, pushing, etc. Some ad-libs are necessary to convey the magnitude of this incident as MOM pulls them apart and brings SIS up front.)

DON.	SIS.
Mom, she hit me in the head.	Did not. Mom, he's making it up.

MOM. I don't want to hear it. Donald, you be nice to your sister, and, young lady, come up here right now.

DON. She did… Like this. *(DON hits himself hard with the book to demonstrate.)*

SIS. He hit himself, and then he hit me, right here, look… *(SIS is almost crying and showing her non-existent bruise to MOM and puts her head on MOM's lap and holds her head as if DON hit her. Some SIS ad-libs are needed to round this moment out.)*

DAD. Be still! Be still.

DON. Dad, I'm not lying, she hit me. *(DON hits himself with book again.)*

DAD. All right, you want something to cry about, son…I can give you something to cry about, now sit!

DON. But I didn't…

MOM. Enough!

DON. But Dad—

DAD. Sit down, son, or I'll make you sit. *(DON sits in disbelief.)* You should be ashamed of yourself. Nobody likes a bully.

(MOM and DAD are checking to make sure their little girl is OK. DAD drives a few beats in silence.)

DAD *(cont'd)*. Yep, Alaska was purchased in 1867. For a paltry seven million dollars. Now that's a bargain. The deal was made by William H. Seward, Secretary of State, I think under—

(SFX: A Volkswagen Beetle passes by and honks.)

DON. Look, Mom, Dad, look!

DAD. Uh-oh… *(Looking around, smiling, tapping MOM.)* Slug bug. *(MOM smiles and taps DAD back in the arm.*

They smile at each other. SIS is still pouting. DAD smiles and taps SIS.) Slug bug.

SIS *(stands and smiles, tapping MOM)*. Slug bug.

MOM *(taps her back)*. Slug bug.

SIS *(goes to back seat and taps DON)*. Slug bug.

DON *(taps SIS)*. Slug bug.

SIS *(taps DON a little harder)*. Slug bug.

DON *(taps SIS a little harder)*. Slug bug.

SIS. SLUUUUUUUUG bug!

(SIS wallops DON as hard as she can, causing mayhem, and DON grabs SIS by her pigtails. The chaos is broken up as MOM and DAD stand up, each grabbing a kid by the ear and pulling them apart.)

DON & SIS. Ow ow ow ow ow ow ow ow ow ow ow!

MOM.	DAD.
Now, Donald, let go of your sister!	This is unacceptable! Unacceptable! Do you hear me?

MOM. Oh, for heaven's sake! Now I need to hear some reading back there, or I'll have your father pull this car over right now.

(DAD grabs book and opens it as DON transitions. MOM, SIS and DAD exit on DAD's lines.)

DAD. Now that's a good idea. I've got two good readers back there and I haven't heard one story yet. Not one good story yet!

(SFX: Car pass.)

DAD *(cont'd).* Look here, big guy. Now this is fascinating when you think about it. The first story in this book is based on the very place we'll be staying. Now what do you think about that?

DON. I think…

(SFX: Car pass, grandparents music. Lights change as DON transitions to front seat.)

DON *(cont'd).* I think…this was the trip, Dad. Hannibal, Missouri, was, well, Hannibal, Missouri. But Route 78 to Mount Union…this was the trip. You know what I remember most?

(Special on GRANDMA and GRANDPA, stepping out behind a gate. They seem frozen. GRANDMA's hands are concealed behind the gate.)

DON *(cont'd).* Driving up and making that turn and seeing Grandma and Grandpa standing there at the gate. *(Pause.)* Like a painting. Waiting. Maybe they heard us and came running out, but it always seemed to me that they had just been standing there, waiting and not moving, for hours. Just waiting, until we'd run up and they'd hand us Krispie treats as big as cement blocks.

GRANDMA. OK, here you go. *(She reveals a plate of giant, cement-block-size Krispie treats.)* Just one now, and make it last. And don't let your grandpa sneak any of it—the sugar gives him the stomach bubbles something awful.

GRANDPA. Hey, kids, I got the tractor fixed yesterday, so I'll need some help stirring up the chickens. Grandma thinks they're getting a little fat. Time to see 'em jump a bit, don't ya think? Who wants to help?

(DON caught in memory half raises his hand.)

GRANDPA *(cont'd).* Well then, maybe you could tear off Grandpa a little piece of that there Krispie treat and I'll see what I can do.

DON. Driving tractors, giant Krispie treats and jumping chickens. Grandpa was the Willy Wonka of Iowa.

(GRANDMA and GRANDPA exit. SFX: Car pass. MOM, DAD and SIS enter with lines. DON hands DAD the steering wheel. They're approaching GRANDMA's house.)

DAD. C'mon now, c'mon...

SIS. Dad, tell Grandpa to let me ride the tractor first? Don went first last time...

DON. She went first last time. I know she did!

DAD. OK OK OK OK, now listen up. I want everyone and I mean everyone on their absolute best behavior, all right? Your absolute best, ya hear? These are old people we're dealing with here, so no roughhousing.

SIS. Mom, if we're good, can we stay an extra night?

MOM. We'll see, sweetheart, ask your father later.

SIS. Dad, if we're good can we stay an extra night?

DAD. Honey, ask your mother again later.

SIS. Mom, if we're good can we stay an extra night?

DAD. All right now that's enough. Hey hey hey, look what I see, look look look who's here...

DON & SIS *(in a flurry of excitement)*. Grandma! Grand-pa!

(The KIDS jump out. SIS makes windmill arms.)

SIS. Grandma, look at me! Look what I can do. I'm a windmill with wings.

(As the rest of the FAMILY exits, DON has picked up the urn and lags behind, beginning to transition.)

DAD. All right, now you heard what I said.

MOM.	DAD.
No empty hands, kids. Grab something and remember what your father said.	Remember, these are old people we're dealing with. Old people. So no rough-housing! These are old people!

(DON takes off his cap and looks around confused, holding the urn. SFX: PA announcement.)

PA. Attention shoppers, potted plants two for one, all potted plants two for one. Thank you, have a nice day.

(A grocery cart lazily rolls onto the stage. An employee rushes out to stop it.)

CART GUY. Whoa whoa whoa! Mobile One to base, we got a runaway cart in sector three. I am sorry about that, sir. We've got a little bit of a slope here and the carts seem to have a mind of their own. They just keep coming and coming and coming and coming and coming and coming. Nothing I can do except push it right back where it came from. I wouldn't stand here, 'cuz it's the low point. You can't see it, but it's there, it's about a 23-, 24-, maybe 25-degree pitch starting right over there at Center Cart Corral, and it slopes all the way down to about where you're standing right there. It slopes. It slopes down and you can hardly see it, but it slopes down, slopes right on down to where you are standing and that would be the low point. Three times they tried to fix it and they still didn't get it right. We did the exact same kind of job for my uncle Terry's driveway with a handmixer and a two by four. Took about three days and a couple of colas but I'm telling ya—you put a shopping cart in the middle of that puppy and it would be waiting there for ya in the morning...but what can you do...it slopes, slopes right down.

DON. A grocery store? Are you kidding me? My grand-mother's house is a grocery store?!

CART GUY. OK, then, you have a nice day, sir. *(Walkie-talkie with his exit.)* Mobile One to base, all carts are clear, coming in checkpoint three and out, but we have a a bit of a crazy man out here in the parking lot.

DON *(incredulous).* A grocery store?

(SFX: Phone rings. SFX: Phone call music. Special on OLDER MOM as she enters and stands, talking out in a phone conversation.)

OLDER MOM. No, no, not too busy...

(OLDER SIS enters stirring a bowl.)

OLDER MOM *(con't)*. Still getting ready. So you made it? Made good time. And how did the, uh, the—the—placement of the... Oh, not yet? I see. OK, well, then I should let you go do that...Thank you for doing this. We feel better about this already and I'm sure your father does, too. It was time.

SIS. Tell him if he's late for dinner he's dead. *(Exits.)*

OLDER MOM. That was your sister...well, just in case. So go ahead, tell me, I can take it, what's it look like? Is it still that God-awful yellow? *(Long pause.)* Green? Green? Oh no, green? Oh, for heaven's sake. Why would they paint it green? What has gotten into people? What was wrong with the yellow? I didn't like it, but at least it wasn't green. Oh, for heaven's sake, green?

(MOM exits. Lights back up on DON.)

DON. I couldn't tell her over the phone. Better to think it's green than know it's a grocery store. *(Pause.)* A grocery store. That didn't feel right. I couldn't leave you there— "Father finally returns home, aisle four next to kitty litter"—just didn't feel right. But if not a grocery store then where?

(DAD comes bounding across the stage. The FAMILY follows, confused but energized, until all stand at roadside looking at a sign.)

DAD. Here it is, kids! Fascinating! Here it is! You betcha, here it is! Historical Marker 223, the Malta Seedling Mile. Fascinating!

(They move away leaving DAD by himself.)

SIS. It's a metal plate stuck on a stick in the middle of no-
    where, and I'm hungry!
DON. Me too…

(The KIDS slump on MOM.)

MOM. Sweetheart, the kids are hungry.
DAD *(still focused on the sign)*. In a minute, dear. It says
    here it was a former dirt road that became one of the
    first experiments in the use of concrete for roads. The
    Lincoln Highway was the first transcontinental hard sur-
    face roadway in America…

(Lights fading to black during next line.)

DAD *(cont'd)*. It was 3,384 miles long from New York
    City to San Francisco. Fascinating, just fascinating…

*(Lights out. Lights up. The KIDS are lying on the
    ground.)*

DAD *(cont'd)*. In 1912, after the investment from President
    William Taft, the first of four seedling miles passed this
    very site. *(Keeps reading to himself, commenting aloud.)*
SIS. Mo-o-om, why are we here?
MOM. You know your father enjoys this.
DON. Why?
MOM. Because he loves history.
DON. Why?
MOM. Because he's your father.

DON. How'd that happen?

MOM. Now stop it! *(Gets camera out of bag knowing DAD will want a picture.)*

DAD. Wow. Think about that. Right here. Right where we're standing. The Malta Seedling Mile.

DON & SIS. DAD! Please! Let's go!

DAD. OK, OK, honey, get a picture of…

(MOM takes picture of DAD and sign. SFX: Picture sound.)

DAD *(cont'd)*. OK, now just the road.

MOM. Sweetheart, the road?

DAD. Yes, the Seedling Mile here. Take a picture.

(MOM takes picture of road. SFX: Picture sound.)

DAD *(cont'd)*. Hey hey hey, and while we're at it, one with the kids! *(Gathers KIDS up for a forced picture.)* Yes yes yes, c'mon quick, don't make that face, it'll stay that way. Let's go, no complaints…

(The KIDS begrudgingly shuffle into the picture.)

DAD *(cont'd)*. Think about that, kids, right where we are standing. The Malta Seedling Mile.

MOM. C'mon, Don, smile, honey. Ready, one, two, three.

MOM, DAD, SIS, DON. Brownings are unpredictable!

(SIS makes a face to ruin the picture. DON is frozen slumped for a moment. SFX: Picture sound. The FAM-

ILY freezes. DON begins after a beat, the FAMILY stays in freeze.)

DON. A mile marker, I suppose was one option. Or a rest stop. You never met one of those you didn't like. I could take you back to Boston and never tell anyone… that feels bad. I could turn around and head on home, but that feels wrong. OK, I admit it, feeling a little lost here, Dad…yep, a little off track.

(SFX: Car pass and field noise. FAMILY transitions out of freeze. The KIDS and MOM head back into the car with lines. DAD is looking out and around.)

DAD. OK, I admit it, we're lost, are you happy now?

MOM. I'm no help without a mile marker.

DAD. OK, OK, OK, tell you what. I'm going to run into this farmhouse here and get us back on track.

DON & SIS. No, Dad, please. Mom, don't let him. It's so hot.

MOM. Sweetheart, are you sure anyone's home?

DAD. Pfft, it's the country. Where would they go?

SIS. Let's just keep driving. Mom?

MOM. Just don't take long, sweetheart.

DAD. I'll be right back.

SIS. Mom, he's lying! Don't let him! Think about us!

MOM. Now stop it.

SIS. Let's just leave him here.

MOM. He'll be back in a minute.

SIS. But it's so-o-o-o ho-o-o-ot!

(Lights up on DAD, standing and talking to JOE HO-FINGERS, a very haggard farmer with a hoe.

SFX: Hot presence—crickets, cicadas, distant tractor.)

DON. Mom, who's Dad talking to?

SIS. She doesn't know.

DON. Shut up! *(Shove.)*

SIS. You shut up. *(Shove.)*

MOM. Just be still.

DON. Be still, her best advice. Be still, conserve water, and watch flies melt on the dashboard.

SIS. Mom, aren't you hot?

MOM. Now, stop it.

DON. That's right, stop it and watch Dad talk to the scary farmer on the hottest day in July because you know the old saying, if the heat doesn't kill you, the scary man with the hoe surely will. Mom? What's he holding? What is it?

SIS. What's it matter?

MOM. It looks like a hoe.

DON. Mom, he's going inside.

(DAD and JOE HOFINGERS disappear.)

SIS. Mom, stop him. He'll stay there and talk forever. Go get him.

DON. No.

SIS. Please go get him.

DON. No-o-o-o, Mom may be all we have left.

SIS *(pleading)*. Mom.

MOM. Just stop. He won't be long.

SIS. Why won't you just get him?

DON. And when she's gone, then we're slave children to the crazy hoe-murdering farmer, did ya ever think of that?

(DAD reappears with FARMER.)

DON *(cont'd)*. There he is, here comes Dad.

MOM. That wasn't long, now was it?

DON. Mom. *(Pause.)* Are you sure that's a hoe?

MOM. I can't tell, sweetheart.

SIS. Yeah, with an extra-sharp edge for cutting.

DON. What?

(SIS notices DON is a little scared. DAD and FARMER meander toward the car.)

MOM. Cut it out.

SIS. Don, look, he's coming over.

DON. What?

SIS. Oh my God, he's bringing the hoe.

MOM. Stop scaring your brother.

DON. I'm not scared.

SIS *(excitedly)*. Don Don Don! He's missing fingers! *(SFX: Scary music. Music and lights change.)* All of them. No fingers! Roll up the windows!

DON.	SIS.
HE'S MISSING FINGERS! MOM, NO FINGERS!	Lock the doors, look the doors, Mom, for Don, lock the doors!

*(SIS has climbed on top of DON and the three climax
the yelling in a dramatic clinch as MOM shouts them
down. DAD and JOE HOFINGERS arrive at the car as
the music and mayhem cuts out.)*

MOM. Nobody IS MISSING ANY FINGERS! *(Music out,
lights back to normal.)*

DAD. Hey, kids, this is Mr. Hofingers, Mr. Joe Hofingers.
(Pause.) His uncle was part Cherokee and he tells me
some of this farm is built on an ancient burial ground.
Right where we are standing. You want to check it out?

DON & SIS. Mom!

MOM. Honey—

DAD. OK, she's right. Thanks again, Joe, really enjoyed it.
And don't forget, if you're ever in Winterset, stop on by.

JOE *(faintly)*. Hmm, Home a the Duke...

(DAD and JOE shake hands. DAD returns to car.)

DAD. Yeah, you are not going to believe the little turn we
missed back there.

MOM *(impatiently)*. We have been burning up out here!

(SFX: Car start.)

DAD *(oblivious)*. Yep, it's a hot one! It's time to turn on
some air! Hey, big guy, check this out. *(Flips an arrowhead back to DON.)*

DON. Wow.

DAD. Joe had an arrowhead collection he wanted me to
see. You know, probably hasn't had a visitor in years.
Nice guy, though. *(Pause.)* Heck of a collection.

MOM. Do we know where we're going?

DAD *(laughs)*. Do we know where we're going? *(To DON.)* Pretty nice, huh?

SIS. Lemme see. *(Grabs the arrowhead.)*

DON. No, give it back! *(Disbelief.)* Mom!

SIS. I did not… *(Keeps denying.)*

(MOM and DAD stand up and go to the back to handle the skirmish prior to the freeze.)

DON. She took my arrowhead! Dad, she took my arrowhead.

DAD. Sweetpea?

DON. Dad, I know she took it!

MOM. Did you take it? If you took it, you need to give it back.

SIS. But I don't have it…

DAD. Now you heard your mother. If you took it, sweetpea, you should give it back!

SIS. But, Dad!

(All freeze. DON speaks.)

DON. All right, big decision here.

(MOM, SIS and DAD continue their same lines as they exit. DON casually heads back to sit in the car. DAD trails a bit and pauses to look at DON when DON says "lie to MOM" and then he exits.)

DON *(cont'd)*. Big decision. If we're going to make the dinner, I turn around right now and figure out what to say when I get there. Or call up Mom, tell her the truth. Hold on. Or, miss the dinner, lie to Mom and keep driving. That's right I said lie to Mom. *(Pause.)* Yep, I say we put this to a family vote.

(SFX: Phone rings. MOM enters.)

MOM. What? Oh no, the car won't start? And you tried to pump it one, two, three? Oh well, I'm glad you're safe, but I'm sick, just sick about you missing the dinner tonight, and your sister—

DON. I know, I know, she's not going to be happy and will want me dead, I know, I know. Look, Mom, tell her I'm miserable, that should make her happy. And tell everyone I'm sorry for missing dinner, and that I said hi. And tell Sis I am sorry I left her alone with Uncle Phil—

(UNCLE PHIL enters and motions to phone.)

MOM. Well, OK, but your uncle Phil wants to talk to you—

DON. Mom, no...

MOM. He's right here. Uncle Phil?! *(She motions.)* And he's been dying to talk to you.

UNCLE PHIL. Is that Don!? Is that DONNY?! *(Rushes to phone.)*

DON. Mom, please, no, no, NO, NO, NO, NO, NO, NO...

UNCLE PHIL. Hey there, Big Time!

DON. Hey, Uncle Phil.

UNCLE PHIL. Hey, Phyllis, get over here. It's Donny.

(AUNT PHYLLIS runs over to phone. She shouts into the phone next to UNCLE PHIL.)

AUNT PHYLLIS. Hey, hey, Donny, go-o-o Hawkeyes, how about it!?

UNCLE PHIL.	AUNT PHYLLIS.
How 'bout them Hawks!? And, boy, how's the news- paper biz going? We're all proud of you back here, very proud very proud very proud indeedy.	Yep, yep. Very proud. Proudy proud proud. Yep, yep, so proud.

UNCLE PHIL. I'm doing better now. Came down with just an awful, awful case of the gout.

AUNT PHYLLIS. Your cousin Rhonda stepped on a nail, had to get a tetanus shot.

UNCLE PHIL. Yep, tell me, have you ever had a case of the gout?

AUNT PHYLLIS. She's fine now.

UNCLE PHIL. Cut it off! That's what I told 'em, cut it off!

(DON snaps his cell phone shut. SFX: Car pass.)

DON. I know it seems like I hung up on them, because I did. *(Pause, drive.)* I need some time to think. I need to stop, think and drink. I need some advice. *(Pause.)* Hey, you remember Jack Singer? Sure you do, Dad. Jack Singer was the first friend I can ever remember having opinions. Opinions that made you think about life and what you were doing with it. He'd say things like, "This place is killing me. I can't wait to get out of this Godforsaken hellhole." That was in third grade. Jack's a professor at Iowa now, very bitter, cynical, angry. *(Pause.)* God, I hope he hasn't changed.

(SFX: Car pass. JACK SINGER enters with a couple beers, ranting.)

JACK SINGER. I hate 'em! I hate 'em, Don! I hate 'em I hate 'em I hate 'em I hate 'em I hate 'em I hate 'em I hate 'em. I do, I can't help it. I hate my students, every single one of 'em. Little pretentious peckerheads! They say it's college, but it feels like kindergarten to me.

(DON is out of the car, accepting a beer.)

JACK SINGER *(cont'd).* Boy, a grocery store, that's a tough one.

DON. Yeah.

JACK SINGER. I try to like these kids. I try. But, I just can't. It's wrong, isn't it? Tell me.

DON. I don't think so.

JACK SINGER. The worst thing of all is this—this—this...dull, lifeless look in their eyes. No, not dull—dead. Just as dead as dead gets. You ever hit a deer?

DON. No.

JACK SINGER. Me neither, but that's the look I'm talking about, Don, that's the look.

DON. Jack, you have no idea how good it is to see you.

JACK SINGER. I swear, Don, I swear, you know my dog will sit and stare into the fan for hours on end. Just sit and stare for hours and I'm telling you, the look I see in his eyes is twice as interested as the one I'm getting back from my students. Am I boring, Don? Do I bore you? Is this boring?

DON. Feeling better already, Jack.

JACK SINGER. We were not this shallow, Don, we were not this shallow. We were stupid, but we were not this shallow. Right?

DON. I guess so.

JACK SINGER *(ranting)*. No soul. They got no soul, Don. They have no soul. No soul, Don, no soul! They just want the degree but they don't want an education. It's about getting someplace as fast as they can and when they get there, they don't even know why they've arrived, or how they got there. They just don't know, Don. They don't. They don't know anything about what they think they know, about anything you're supposed to know. Or have traveled to find out to know. You know?

DON. I think so.

JACK SINGER. Well thank God somebody does. Thank God there's somebody. 'Cause I'm not sure if I know. Boy, a grocery store, that's a tough one. Any ideas where you're gonna…

DON. No, not yet. I was thinking about turning around but that doesn't feel right, at least not yet.

JACK SINGER. Yeah, that's a tough one.

DON. My dad was a lot of things, but he wasn't a quitter. Is your dad still alive?

JACK SINGER. Yeah, kinda. Boy, that's a tough one. Don, don't beat yourself up over this, old boy. That there guilt's a tricky thing, my friend, a tricky, tricky thing. Driven some men to drink, even worse, others to quit.

DON. You're probably right.

JACK SINGER. Yeah well, who knows? Maybe you're on some kind of damned adventure.

DON. I hope so, Jack, boy, I hope so.

(SFX: Hannibal music. FAMILY enters. SIS leads, running in.)

SIS. Dad, what are we doing? Where are we going?

DAD. OK, OK, looks like we are a little over halfway to Hannibal. We got a little sidetracked, but that's why we take trips like these for adventures like this. So we're here, let's take the rest of the day and just have fun. So, what do you think, dear?

MOM. I might check out some stores on Main Street and just wander around a bit.

SIS. What about you, Dad?

DAD. Well, I'm thinking about checking out this cemetery of war heroes and maybe catch a guided tour of the historical village square in town. So, who's going with who?

SIS. I'll go with, Dad.

MOM & DAD. Don?

DON. So let's see, shopping in the vicinity of people, commerce, maybe a pinball machine, or visiting unknown dead people. I'll go with… *(Pause.)* Mom.

DAD. All right, so say we meet back here about 4:30 or so…

SIS. Dad, hurry, we'll be late. *(Pulls DAD offstage running.)*

DAD. It's a cemetery, sweetpea, they're not going anywhere.

DON. But it never worked out. Never. Instead, we would stumble upon—

MOM *(takes his hand and starts walking)*. Oh look, Don!

(A MAN and WOMAN enter, holding up a quilt.)

DON. The old traveling Amish flea market.

(SFX: Amish music. The quilt drops revealing an AMISH COUPLE.)

AMISH GUY. Hello, ma'am. What makes this one special is the weave.

AMISH GAL. It's a family weave.

AMISH GUY. It's a secret.

AMISH GAL. None like it, you know.

MOM. Beautiful.

AMISH GUY. Forty years to make this quilt.

AMISH GAL. Forty years. None like it, you know.

MOM. Just beautiful. Isn't it beautiful, Don?

AMISH GUY. Thank you, ma'am.

MOM. And what are these?

AMISH GAL. These, well, these are wind chimes.

AMISH GUY. Made from petrified Apache toenails.

AMISH GAL. Hard as stone, none like it, you know.

AMISH GUY. Well over two hundred years old.

MOM. Don, look at that. Well I have never…petrified toenails?

(COUPLE gathers quilt and begins to exit.)

AMISH GUY. That's right, ma'am, and if you have time I hope you can join us in the west meadow.

AMISH GAL. There's a pie-tasting.

AMISH GUY. Three years to make those pies.

AMISH GAL. None like 'em, you know. *(They exit.)*

DON. The only thing that made moments like these bearable was knowing my sister was stuck looking at second-string dead generals.

(SIS and DAD enter, rushed and breathless.)

SIS. Omigod! Omigod! Omigod! You're not going to believe this!

DAD. Sorry we're late.

MOM. Oh my Lord, what happened?

SIS. There was this man and he was dangling from the top of this building!

MOM. Where did you take her?

DAD. On the tour, but the craziest thing, the streets were roped off!

SIS. Yeah, and the fire truck had to put the ladder bucket all the way up—how high, Dad?

DAD. At least fifty feet.

SIS. And he's hanging from these poles—

MOM. Who?

DAD. Eh, scaffolding. *(To MOM.)* Oh, he's fine.

SIS. Yeah, and he's swinging back and forth!

MOM. Oh, goodness!

DAD. He's fine, he's fine.

MOM. What happened to the cemetery?

DAD. Closed.

MOM.	DON.
What?	What?

DAD. Yep, no more tours because of the new go-cart track they built next to it. Kind of sad.

(DON looks out to audience.)

SIS. They have four tracks, Don! It's so cool.

DAD. She's a little Richard Petty.

SIS. I lapped you twice.

DAD. Oh, I was too full from ice cream to race.

DON *(drops his head)*. Ice cream? Ice cream? Every time. Every single time! She returns with fun fun fun tales of fun people having fun!

(SFX: Car pass. Lights change. DAD looks at local tour map again.)

DAD. Well, let's see here...I'm not sure I can top this morning's adventure with sweetpea, but let's see. Hey, look here, a Civil War show. And hey! There's a bayonet demonstration. Anybody else?

MOM. There's an art fair outside of town. Leave me there.

SIS. I'll go with Mom.

MOM & DAD. Don?

DON. I'll go with...I'll go with... *(Pause, take to audience, then somewhat resigned.)* I'll go with Dad.

DAD. OK then, let's go, big guy. This should be fascinating!

DON *(a quick take with a sigh.)*

(Blackout. In the darkness, we hear the next line.)

CIVIL WAR GUY *(loudly)*. Boom. Boom. Boom!

(Lights up on CIVIL WAR GUY, dressed in Civil War garb with a musket and bayonet and a MUSEUM ASSISTANT. DAD and DON are now finding their seats. NOTE: Often it works for them to be seated in the audience.)

CIVIL WAR GUY *(cont'd)*. Boom. Boom. Boom! Imagine, if you will, that it is midnight and you have just heard those shots being fired from an enemy musket.
MUSEUM ASSISTANT *(reading from a note card)*. Welcome, everyone, to the two o'clock historical narrative of Lieutenant Dan Meechum. Please, no flash photography or talking during the performance. Thank you. Bathrooms are out the door and to the left over that way. Thank you. *(MUSEUM ASSISTANT exits.)*
CIVIL WAR GUY. Hi, I'm Lieutenant Dan Meechum. *(Listens for response from audience. Forcefully this time:)* Soldiers! I will say it again, "Hi, I'm Lieutenant Dan Meechum." *(Audience response.)* Very good. And I, Lieutenant Dan, was born in Raleigh, North Carolina. I fought in the Civil War in 1862 and I'm here to tell you about my amazing experiences with General Robert E. Lee. But first may I request a volunteer enemy combatant to assist in a simple but deadly bayonet strike to the midsection?

(DAD volunteers enthusiastically while DON tries unsuccessfully to pull his hand down.)

DON.	DAD.
Dad, please. Please.	It's OK, son.

CIVIL WAR GUY. Very well then. You, sir. *(DAD runs up to the stage.)* How you doing today, sir?

DAD. Private Browning reporting for service.

CIVIL WAR GUY. Very good, Private.

DAD. I've left my only son at home to take care of the family as so many brave soldiers did. Lieutenant Meechum, that's my boy Donny right over there.

DON *(embarrassed)*. DA-A-D-D!

CIVIL WAR GUY. Everything OK?

DAD. He's fine. I think he has to tinkle.

DON. DAAADDD! *(DON ducks in embarrassment.)*

CIVIL WAR GUY. Very good then. And please stand right here, sir.

(DAD waves to his son. CIVIL WAR GUY acts out his monologue with great intensity and flair. NOTE: Over-the-top blocking is encouraged.)

CIVIL WAR GUY *(cont'd)*. Back in 1863 the musket was a flawed, imperfect weapon and many men met their fate at the end of a bayonet. It would have been a swift, *(demonstrates an exaggerated, swift motion with musket at the audience with sound)* forceful, *(another movement with sound, more exaggerated than the first)* and violent strike. *(The final, most exaggerated movement and sound.)* So violent, so terribly, terribly violent *(hands DAD the musket who aims it at CIVIL WAR GUY, who then takes tennis ball out of pocket, places on tip of bayonet. CIVIL WAR GUY pulls the end of the bayonet into his stomach grasping the tennis ball as DAD pulls the musket back.)* His feet would have left the ground, *(a small hop)* and then in a matter of seconds, *(he stammers)* the harsh, harsh *(stammers again)* bloody reality *(stammers yet again)* of war would set in.

(He falls and lays motionless. DAD takes tentative steps toward the motionless body. DAD raises the gun, silently victorious to the crowd. DON stands.)

DON *(whispers).* Dad, we're going to be late.
CIVIL WAR GUY *(lurches up).* One man dies, another lives; the numbers sacrificed are unknown but the solider's sacrifice, *(retrieves gun from DAD)* the soldier's sacrifice should never be forgotten.

(SFX: Civil War music.)

DAD. Wow! Outstanding! *(Claps.)* Outstanding! Huh, what do you think about that, son? Outstanding!

(Lieutenant Meechum salutes. DAD salutes back with great patriotism. Lieutenant Meechum marches off.)

DAD *(cont'd).* Outstanding! Simply outstanding!

(They salute each other. CIVIL WAR GUY exits. MUSEUM ASSISTANT enters.)

MUSEUM ASSISTANT. The next historical narrative is at four p.m. Bathrooms are to the left. You may now take pictures.

DON *(pleading)*. Dad, can we go now?

DAD. One second, big guy. Excuse me, ma'am, can I ask you a favor? Could you take a picture of me and my boy here? *(DAD hands MUSEUM ASSISTANT a camera.)*

DON. Dad.

DAD *(pulls DON into the photo)*. Now, don't be that way. Take your hat off and stand up straight and salute, son, like Lieutenant Dan.

(SFX: Picture sound. The sound accents the light change. DAD and DON freeze on DAD's over-the-top salute. A beat as the lights change to a night setting. MUSEUM ASSISTANT exits. SFX: Car pass. DON breaks away to the driver's seat.)

DON. Boy, you never see stars like this, not in the city. Well, Dad, Jack asked me to spend the night, but I told him I had to push on. He told me not to be too hard on myself, but I'm not sure how to do that.

(Lights close in on DON driving deep into the night.)

DON *(cont'd., to the urn)*. You gave us everything and asked for nothing and even when we tried to say thank you, "Oh no, no, no, you go thank your mother." Even Christmas, Christmas! The most we could ever get, if we were lucky, was a request for some new socks or under-wear. Do you understand what's wrong with that? You can't live an entire life and only ask for new socks and underwear. And now I have a chance to finally honor what may have been your one and only request, and it's a grocery store?! It's not fair. It's not. It's not fair.

(SFX: Car pass and loud honk. MOM and SIS enter car.
DAD moves to the driver's seat, DON to back seat. They
pass the steering wheel off on their lines.)

DAD. It's just not fair, it's not fair.
MOM. Honey, please.
DAD. Damn RVs!

(SFX: DAD honks.)

DAD *(cont'd)*. Those RVs are nothing but big hazards on
   wheels. Dammit, make a turn.

(SFX: DAD honks.)

MOM. Honey, no honking. It only makes matters worse.
DAD. We have a home, do we feel the need to slap wheels
   on it and cart it all over the country? No! Bunch of
   waste. Bunch of big fat hazards and a big fat waste.
   What the heck is he doing?!
MOM. Honey, just relax.
DAD. Sweetheart, this is ridiculous. I can't get around him.
MOM. Sweetheart, remember what Pastor John says, prac-
   tice patience, dear. He'll turn soon.
DAD. He's not turning, and Pastor John doesn't have a
   driver's license, that's why he can talk like that. Honey,
   they don't belong on these roads. *(Out the window.)*
   Move your double-wide ass over, ya wide load!
SIS. Mom, Dad said ass.
MOM. Language! Sweetheart, language.

DAD. I'm not going to sit here all day. We need to try and get around him. *(Determined.)* Honey, I'm making my move.

MOM. Sweetheart?

DAD. That's OK, I got 'im.

(DAD leans out the window, repeating "I got 'im." DON and SIS stand and are moving over DAD's shoulder. MOM is grabbing DAD's shoulder, yelling also. SFX: Engine accelerating.)

FAMILY *(yelling)*. DAD DAD DAD DAD DAD NO NO NO AHHHHH!

DAD.	FAMILY.
I think we got 'im—we	DAD DAD DAD DAD
got 'im—we got 'im—	D-A-A-A-A-A-A-A-A-A-D—

(The FAMILY and sound freezes.)

DON. More than once I felt my life flash before my eyes as we faced off in a death match with an oncoming semi. While the RV may have tormented you, I must admit, these moments made our trips truly, well, I have to say, fascinating.

(SFX: Loud horn blast. Truck passing by. DON pops back into position and the FAMILY continues yelling, physically swaying with the swerving car. DAD is now in front of the RV, narrowly missing the semi. SIS and MOM are breathless and almost unable to speak. DON is excited, almost proud.)

DAD. Ha ha! That'll show him. Had him by a mile. Adios, amigos!

DON. Adios, amigos!

MOM. Sweetheart, that was close. A little close.

DAD. Had him by a mile.

DON. By a mile, Dad, a mile.

SIS. Mom, I think I'm going to be sick.

MOM. Breathe a little, you'll be fine, sweetheart. Deep breaths.

DAD. Had 'im by a mile.

DON. He had 'im by a mile, Mom.

(DON sits back down. Lights change as the moment barely settles. SFX: Tractor sound rolls in.)

MOM. Oh no, a tractor.

DAD. Check this out, kids. Kids, look at that old sonofa-gun.

(The KIDS stand behind MOM and DAD.)

DAD *(cont'd).* Now that's the life right there, you betcha.

MOM. Go around him. He's going so slow.

DAD. Just taking his time, dear. Just taking his time.

MOM. Now there's a hazard for you.

DAD. Oh, no, sweetheart. Oh no. Right there, right there, kids, that's the backbone of this country. That's the backbone.

DON. Whenever you talked about backbone, I bought it hook, line and sinker.

DAD. That farmer right there on that tractor—take a good look—the best part of this country. You betcha, you betcha.

DON. Toss in a simple "You betcha" and suddenly we weren't just seeing some old fart, or some old man on a tractor, but we were seeing some kind of damned American old fart of a hero on a tractor, just like you read about in *Reader's Digest*. And it made you feel, well, good.

(DAD starts "This Land Is Your Land" with a very quiet "Bum bum bum bum bum, bum bum bum bum bum." MOM and SIS join in.)

DON *(cont'd)*. And if only for a brief moment, it gave us hope, hope that maybe this year it would be different. That maybe this time we wouldn't get too lost and maybe this year we could arrive on time—

(CIVIL WAR GUY, AMISH GAL appear and join in.)

SIS. Dad, are you sure there's a pool?

DAD. You betcha, sweetpea, you betcha.

DON. And maybe there would be pools without hazardous levels of toxic chemicals.

MOM. Has anyone seen a mile marker? *(Stands and moves next to SIS.)*

DON. And maybe the home of Mark Twain would truly be something to behold.

DAD. This is going to be fascinating, just fascinating. *(Stands and moves next to DON.)*

DON. And wherever we were going, and whenever we got there, it was OK, because we were going there with Mom and Dad as the Unpredictable Browning Family, survivors of a near-fatal head-on collision, you betcha, you betcha!

(The FAMILY freezes, music stops. DON moves to the driver's seat of the car.)

DON *(cont'd)*. And maybe Jack was right. Maybe, just maybe I was on some kind of damned adventure and maybe I shouldn't turn around and bury you in the back-yard with some new tube socks and underwear. And maybe, just maybe this could be the best trip ever.

(FAMILY sings again as lights fade. SFX: Intermission announcement.)

END OF ACT I

ACT II

(SFX: Loud thunder, the sound of rain. Lights on DON. SFX: Flooded car, not starting. DON is talking and muttering to the car, trying to coax it to start.)

CAR.	DON *(to the car)*.
NNNNNNNNNNNNNN	C'mon, c'mon, c'mon. Talk to
NNNNNNNNNNNNNN.	me, talk to me, talk to me, talk
NNNNNNNNNNNNNN	to me.

DON *(cont'd)*. OK, listen to me. Yes, I get it. Lie to Mom about the car not starting and now the car won't start. So, OK, let's try it your way, Mom. One, two, three and—

(SFX: Flooded car, not starting.)

DON *(cont'd)*.	CAR.
C'mon, c'mon, c'mon.	NNNNNNNNNNNNNNNNN
I think I can, I think I	NNNNNNNNNNNNNNNNN
can, I think I can,	NNNNNNNNNNNNNNNNN

DON *(cont'd, exasperated)*. I think I cannot believe this! I cannot believe this is happening! *(Bolts from car and paces and takes out phone.)* You know what I oughtta do? You know what I oughtta do? I should stop the first

RV that comes by and say, "Here, take him. Just take him."

(Lights change. The FAMILY enters car, MOM drives. DAD is in passenger seat.)

DON *(con'd)*. He'd never admit it, but it's what he wanted. It's what he wanted. Yep, making some good time now...

(SFX: Car pass. DON joins the car and starts playing cat in the cradle with SIS.)

DAD. Making some good time, honey...

DON *(overlap)*. ...making some good time now.

DAD. Making good time, honey. Now that seat may need some adjustment there. *(Reaches over to adjust the seat, but MOM pushes him away. DAD has the traveler's guide open.)*

MOM. Yes, I've got it, dear.

DAD. Here, let me—

MOM. I've got it.

DAD. Check the mirrors. Ya know, more accidents are caused by not doing the little things. *(DAD now has his head completely in front of MOM's vision.)*

MOM. Honey, your head, I can't see.

DAD. Just trying to get the mileage here, hon.

MOM. I can't see.

DAD. OK, time for a little Browning vacation mileage update. Now let's see, we're here, so we have traveled... fascinating. Careful now, dear, there might be speed traps up ahead. I'd keep it at 50, 55 tops.

MOM. I've got it, sweetheart.

DAD. Now last year we averaged almost two miles less per gallon over approximately the same distance, similar weather conditions. Do the math, and that works out to, wow, a savings of almost three cents a mile. I'll need to check some old guides when we get home but I think we may be on our way to a record. *(Looking back.)* Uh-oh, honey, looks like we've got an RV trying to get by us here. *(Adjusts rearview mirror to see approaching RV.)*

MOM. Sweetheart, now I can't see. *(Re-adjusts mirror back.)*

DAD. That's OK, *(re-adjusting mirror back again)* I got it. Yep, wide load trying to pass on the left. Just don't let him in.

MOM. I think that's so rude.

DAD. That's OK, just don't slow down.

MOM. You said 55 tops.

DAD. I know, but go ahead and punch it. Let's see what she's got.

MOM. I'm trying, but honey, he's right on top of us.

DAD. That's why you gotta punch it. Honey, honey, he's making his move. You gotta punch it.

SIS. C'mon, Mom.

DON. Go ahead, Mom.

DAD. Not feeling the punch, sweetie. In fact I'd say you're slowing down. You need some punch—

MOM. He's speeding up!

DAD. No, you're slowing down!

MOM. Oh, I am not!

DAD. That's why you gotta punch it. Tell her, kids.

DON & SIS *(getting into the act)*. Yeah, Mom, punch it. Punch it, Mom, punch it! Punch it, Mom, punch it!

(DON and SIS chant underneath MOM and DAD, "Punch it, Mom, punch it. Punch it, Mom, punch it.")

MOM. There's somebody up ahead!

DAD. So let's show 'em what you got, sweetie! Show 'em that you won't back down.

MOM. I don't like this. He's too close.

DAD. That's why you gotta punch it! *(Jumps up.)* Now, sweetie!

DAD, SIS, DON. Now, now, now, now, now, now!

DAD. No, no, no, no, no,

DAD, SIS, DON. Ahhhhhhhh! *(DAD smacks his head and slaps his knee with the map as the FAMILY slumps back in disappointment.)*

MOM. Now just stop it!

DAD. Awwwwww, why didn't you punch it?!

MOM. Now just stop it. There's no way to stop a thing that big. He was right on top of me.

DAD. Well, great, now we're stuck for who knows how long.

MOM. Oh, you do your job and leave me be.

(They drive a beat.)

DAD. Why is he slowing down? He is slowing down on purpose!

MOM. Oh, he is not.

(SIS takes DON's hat.)

DON. Give it back!

DAD. Hey, hey, hey! Who wants to get in trouble back there? Because I am in no mood! No mood. No-o-o mood.

(A quiet tug of war ensues with hat in the back seat. DON delivers his next three lines with quick pauses from the tug of war.)

DON. It only happened once.
DAD. Oh, c'mon. This is ridiculous.
DON. It unfolded like a crime of passion.
DAD. What is he doing? What in the heck is he doing?!
DON. It came to be known as "The Honking Incident."
MOM. He's not doing anything.
DAD. That's right, he's doing nothing. Nothing, he's doing absolutely nothing! Well, I'm doing something!

(SFX: Music: "Carmina Burana." Lights change dramatically emphasizing the slow-motion movements of DAD and the FAMILY. DAD stands up, adjusts his belt with great emphasis and swings his hand up high and comes down on the steering wheel horn. The entire family is in slow motion, following DAD's hand down to the steering wheel with exaggerated expressions: SFX: Loud, long, horn honk. On the honk, the lights return to what they were. DAD stays on the horn another beat or two and then releases, with a few ad-libs, "Take that, will ya," and regular speed ensues. MOM is in an almost quiet, head-shaking rage as DAD shakes his fist out at the RV. DON and SIS are silent as they sit back down, aware of MOM's palpable anger. DAD sits, still gloating, until:)

MOM *(very deliberate)*. Don't you ever, ever do that again.

DAD *(mumbles into traveler's guide)*. Well, they act like they—

MOM. Don't!

DAD *(under breath)*. —like they own the road.

(They drive a beat.)

SIS *(tentative)*. Mom?

MOM. What!?

SIS. I have to go.

MOM. Fine, I'm pulling over anyway. Your father apparently needs to drive!

(MOM hands DAD the steering wheel. MOM grabs bag and exits, upset. SIS follows, saying her line as she exits.)

SIS. Dad got in trouble, Dad got in trouble.

(DAD sets steering wheel down and trails after SIS, then turns around to DON.)

DAD. Whattya you looking at? Go inside there, and check on your mother…and tell her that you love her…and tell her that you're sorry. And then come back and tell me how's she's doing. *(DAD exiting.)* Tell me how it looks, just tell me how it looks!

(Lights change. SFX: Loud overpowering sounds of a garage. DON shouts to be heard. A greasy MECHANIC

enters and leans over the car with a flashlight in his
mouth. He speaks with a series of grunts and noises.)

DON. So how's she doing? How does it look?

MECHANIC *(make these words indistinguishable)*. Boy, it
could be your…or maybe it's your. I'm just not sure until we can take a look at the manifold.

DON. I'm sorry, what did you say?

MECHANIC. Huh? Oh. *(Takes the flashlight out of his*
mouth, straightens up, and repeats the words just as he
did with the flashlight in his mouth.) I said… *(Same in-*
distinguishable sounds.)

DON. I'm sorry.

MECHANIC. Ha! Gotcha! *(Laughing.)* Gets 'em every
time. Jamie in the back taught me that one. She's killer,
absolute killer. Hey, Jamie!

(JAMIE comes out and leans over the engine.)

DON. Any idea how long?

MECHANIC. Yeah, looks like the starter.

JAMIE. Could be, maybe not, don't know.

MECHANIC. Don't know yet.

DON. Any idea how long?

MECHANIC. What?

DON. How long?

JAMIE. Could be a while.

MECHANIC. It might be a while.

JAMIE. Maybe not, won't know.

MECHANIC. So where ya from?

DON. Winterset, ehh, Boston.

MECHANIC. What?

DON. Winterset!

MECHANIC. Hey, Home of the Duke, no kidding. You like impressions?

DON. Not really.

MECHANIC. Well, Jamie does one heck of a John Wayne.

DON. That's OK really…

MECHANIC. Come on, Jamie, let 'er rip. Show 'im what you got. *(JAMIE is hesitant to show off.)* Oh, c'mon now. Seriously, it's a killer, wait till you hear it, go ahead, let 'er rip.

JAMIE. "Where you headed, Pilgrim?" *(JAMIE's not happy with the impression and exits quickly.)*

MECHANIC. Whad I tell you? Pretty good. Do it again. Oh c'mon, Jamie, don't be like that. Don't worry, I'll get 'er. Jamie! Oh c'mon, Jamie!? *(Follows her off.)*

DON *(calls offstage)*. Yeah, that was good. Please, my car? Please… Well, look, how 'bout… Please, my car!

(SFX: Car pass. DON pauses and takes out notepad.)

DON *(cont'd)*. So far on our list of possible resting places we have the mile marker, a rest area, and the RV, which right now all feel like pretty poor fill-ins for Grandma's house.

(Walks over to hotel area and waits for service.)

DON *(cont'd)*. OK, just think, think, think of something… OK, you loved a bargain. You'd drive forty miles for an all-you-can-eat brunch or an early bird special. So maybe I should just find a half-price buffet and leave you there, yeah…

(SFX: Multiple phone rings. CLERK enters with neck brace and one crutch, or a cane, and answers phone.)

CLERK *(on phone).* Hello, Best Stay, where your stay is our best concern, what can I do for you? Excuse me, sir, can I ask you to hold on a minute? Can you hold on a minute? HOLD ON A MINUTE!

(DRUNK LADY approaches in bathrobe with ice bucket.)

CLERK *(cont'd., to DRUNK LADY).* And what can I do for you?

DRUNK LADY. Hey...I ran outta ice and locked myself out... I'm gonna need a key...room 223.

CLERK *(to DON).* And what can I do for you?

DON. My car is broken down and I might need a room and I was wondering—

DRUNK LADY. A key plea— *(To DON.)* HEY, you're cute!

CLERK *(to DON).* Hang on. *(To DRUNK LADY.)* Hang on.

(DRUNK LADY sits on floor and plays with ice.)

CLERK *(cont'd, back to phone).* Yes sir, plenty of rooms left, cleanest rooms in the state, looking forward to it. *(Hangs up.)*

DRUNK LADY. No, wait, room 242...no...

DON. I was also looking for a bite to eat; is the diner still open?

DRUNK LADY. I'm hungry, huh? You and me? *(Wink, wink.)*

(DON grabs some brochures from CLERK's desk.)

CLERK. That's Gabby's, and it sure is.

DRUNK LADY. No, no, it's room 256.

CLERK. I think my cousin Jessie is working tonight, so you're in for a treat.

DON. Thanks. *(Waves brochures.)*

DRUNK LADY. 236.

CLERK. Hey, some of those brochures of local interest might be a little outdated. Sorry 'bout that. *(Grabs brochures from DON.)*

DON. That's OK.

DRUNK LADY *(looking at it)*. Ha…ice is funny, you know?

CLERK. Yep, this one here on top closed down three years ago. Rock Country. They had rocks in the shape of each state. Big, too. Then a piece came off Rhode Island and whacked a kid in the head, closed 'em down just like that. Kid was OK. Damn shame.

DRUNK LADY. Damn shame.

CLERK. Let's see, Candle Gardens is open, Ghost Caverns, I'm pretty sure they're closed. Dandelion Alley, I hear that's pretty, if you like dandelions—

DRUNK LADY. I love dandy-lions.

DON. I'm sorry, what was that last one?

CLERK. Dandelion Alley—

DON. No, before.

CLERK. Ghost Caverns, I think they're closed.

DRUNK LADY *(stands)*. I GOT IT! I GOT IT. It's right here. *(Pulls key out of pocket, holds it up high, she turns to DON.)* Call me. 222, that's right, 222. Seriously... cute!

CLERK. I can call 'em if you want but they're closed.

DRUNK LADY *(exiting)*. 222. Yeah, it's 222.

DON. No, no, that's fine, but can I see that brochure?

CLERK. Sure, take 'em all. Knock yourself out.

(SFX: Swoosh! Lights up on FAMILY in car.)

DON. Ghost Caverns.

CLERK. I'm pretty sure they're closed.

DON. Ghost Caverns, wow.

(SFX: Swoosh!)

CLERK. That's right, closed.

(SFX: Swoosh!)

SIS. Hey—did you see that? Dad, did you see that? Don, did you see it, did you see it? Wait 'til you see it!

(DON transitions to the car.)

DON. See what?

SIS. The billboard! Wait 'til you see it! Dad, if it's on the way, can we, can we, can we... *(Until the sound. SFX: Swoosh!)* There it is, Don! There it is again! LOOK, DON, LOOK!

(SFX: Music: Ghost Caverns chorus. SIS and DON step to light from above, magically pulling them forward.)

DON. The lettering was bold and brilliant, almost 3-D. They called them Ghost Caverns and they were only thirty-four miles away, promising stalagmites the size of giant Christmas trees, with—

SIS. Monster bats and flying witches!

DON & SIS *(look at each other)*. Monster bats and flying witches.

(Lights change back. DON and SIS chant back to car.)

DON & SIS *(cont'd)*. Monster bats and flying witches *(Repeat.)*

(SFX: Swoosh!)

SIS. Dad, if it's on the way can we go? Can we, can we, can we go please?

DAD. Uhh, no.

SIS. But it's only thirty-four miles! Dad?!

DAD. No.

DON. Hey, Dad, if we can't, can we go to the Dells?

DAD. No.

SIS. But why?

DAD. It's not on the way.

SIS. But this one's only thirty-four miles!

DAD. No.

SIS. But why?

DAD. Because no, that's why.

(SFX: Swoosh!)

SIS. Dad, there's another one! Only thirty-four miles away! It's so close! *(Pleading.)* Mom, pleeease pretty pleeeeese pretty pretty pretty please?

MOM. You heard your father.

SIS. Mom, pleeese tell Dad we can go!

DAD. I said no. I even heard me say no. Honey, did you hear me say no?

MOM. I heard you say no.

DAD. In case you didn't hear me, sweetpea, NO.

SIS *(a desperate kid fit)*. But Da-a-a-a-a-a-a-a-a-a-a-d, if we're not going to get to Hannibal tonight, then why not why not why not? Why not?

DAD. How many times do I have to say no before you start to hear the word no?

DON *(flat)*. That's what we were going to find out.

DAD.	SIS.
Well then no and no	But Dad but Dad
and no and no and no	but Dad but Dad
and no and that's final!	but Dad but Dad.
And I mean final!	But Dad, but Dad, but…

(SIS and DON sit back. SIS is pouting, wiping away tears of frustration.)

DON *(to DAD)*. Why you wouldn't admit defeat and save yourself I'll never know, but a line had been drawn, the gauntlet thrown, and a test of wills had begun.

(SIS swells with each of DON's words.)

DON *(cont'd)*. And know this. We shall never give up, never admit defeat, never hear the word no and we will break you, old man, over the next twenty-six miles.

(SFX: Swoosh!)

SIS. Dad, Dad, Dad, it's only twenty-six miles!
DON. Sure you had size, intellect, and a driver's license. But we had my sister, youth, endurance, and—and—

(SFX: Swoosh!)

DON *(cont'd)*. Billboards the size of battleships!
SIS. Da-a-a-a-a-a-a-a-d, did you see that one? Did you s-e-e-e-e-e-e that one?
DAD. Yes, I did.
SIS. Well, then now can we—
DAD. No, we can't.
DON. Are you sure you saw it, Dad?
DAD. Yep.
SIS. Mom, can you please ask Dad? Mom, please ask Dad?
DAD. Don't pester your mother.
SIS. Dad, we won't ask for anything else, really. We really, really, really won't.
DON. Dad, please. C'mon, we won't, we won't!
SIS. Why would we?
DAD. We don't have time. Sorry, gang.

DON.	SIS.
But it's on the wa-a-a-y!	It's on the wa-a-a-y!

DAD. No, no, no, it's far too expensive!

(DON and SIS sit down in defeat. They sit quiet and dejected for several moments and then…SFX: Swoosh!)

DON & SIS. FREE PARKING!

SIS.	DON.
Dad, it said free parking! It's free! Can we now?	Free! Can we now? Please, Dad? It said free! Free!

DAD. Free parking does not mean free.
DON. But it's free.
SIS. But, Dad, if it's free, it's not expensive. It's free.

DAD.	DON & SIS *(chanting)*.
Keep it up. Just keep it up. Just keep it up—keep it up.	It's free, free, free. Free free free free free…

DAD. DID YOU NOT HEAR WHAT I SAID!
DON *(flat)*. You said keep it up.
SIS *(flat)*. And that's what we're going to do.
DON & SIS *(singing together)*. It's free, free, free. Free free free free free free…
DAD. Now I'm warning you!

(DAD starts to protest again, but SIS silences him and gathers herself.)

SIS. Dad, if we stop at Ghost Caverns we'll be good for the rest of the trip.
DON. Yep.
SIS. We'll leave whenever you say.

DON. Yep.

SIS. And we won't ask for anything.

DON. Nope.

SIS. This is why we come on these trips, right? For adventures like these! *(Pause.)* Why can't we go? It wouldn't hurt anybody, and then we would be better the whole trip and not say anything and just stay back here *(pause)* and and and and and and and and... *(she quickly grabs books, sits, pulls DON down, hands him his book)* and read.

DON. Read!?

MOM. Read?

DAD. It's a trick.

DON. Yes! Read! After thirty minutes of non-stop head-rattling, grade-A badgering, and now—read. Brilliant. She was gifted and demanded my respect and admiration.

(SIS and DON sit back and read intently for a beat. On the "swoosh," they look up and badger DAD in unison until he responds. Then they go back to the books, back up on the "swoosh," etc. SFX: Swoosh!)

DON & SIS. Dad, can we can we can we can we can we?

DAD. No!

(SFX: Swoosh!)

DON & SIS. Can we can we can we can we can we?!

DAD. No!

(SFX: Swoosh!)

DON & SIS. CAN WE CAN WE CAN WE CAN WE?!
DAD. NO! Enough! Please! Enough! You kids are driving me crazy!

(The KIDS smack their books closed. DON starts to celebrate. Again, SIS silences DON.)

SIS. Dad? *(Moves in slowly toward DAD.)* Da-a-d? Da-a-d? *(SIS nuzzles against DAD's shoulder, making eyes at him, etc.)* But, Da-a-a-dy, I love you.
DON. I...STOOD...IN...AWE!
DAD *(big breath)*. We'll see.

(KIDS start to react.)

DAD *(cont'd)*. I said we'll see.
DON. "We'll see" were the words of a broken man.
MOM. Honey...
DAD *(pause)*. Oh, all right.

(SFX: Celebration music with lights. The KIDS go running around the car. SIS does a cartwheel, they dance, hug, etc.)

DON & SIS *(jubilant)*. HOOOO-RAYYYYYYYYY!
DAD *(finally gets their attention)*. All right now, listen up! Now here's the deal: one hour.
DON & SIS. OK
DAD. No dilly-dallying.
DON & SIS. OK.
DAD. No snacks and no souvenirs!
DON & SIS. OK.

DAD. No TV until college.

DON & SIS. OK.

DAD. Broccoli and Brussel sprouts for dinner.

DON & SIS. OK.

DAD. And we'll be leaving you in the caves to be raised by ghosts and wild animals.

DON & SIS. OK. We promise, Dad, we promise, we promise.

SIS. That's great, I love wild animals.

DAD. All right then. We are going to Ghost Caverns!

(KIDS celebrate, then settle.)

SIS. Mom, have you ever been in a cave before?

MOM. No, sweetheart. I haven't.

DAD *(squinting)*. So, what's it say up there, turn right?

SIS. It says turn left.

DON. Yeah, Dad, left.

DAD. I thought we were looking for free parking.

SIS. That's left!

DON. Turn left, Dad, left!

MOM. Turn left, honey.

DAD. No, I think the parking is to the right. *(Turns right.)*

DON & SIS. Right, Dad?! Dad? Dad. Dad. We missed it!

DAD. Are you sure?

DON. Yeah, we're sure!

(DON and SIS step out of the car, gesturing.)

DON & SIS. Billboard, big as a battleship, turn left! *(They return to back seat.)*

DAD. No, I think it said right for the free parking.

MOM. Sweetheart, I think it said—

(SFX: Pothole.)

MOM *(cont'd)*. What was that?

(Lights change. SFX: Car bumping along a road. Everyone starts to shake. The following are words to help the actors. Not all need to be said or will even be heard over the SFX.)

MOM *(cont'd)*. thatthatththatathttaht it said ttttttturn lllleft…
SIS. No-o-o-o-o-o-o-o, Daadddddd, Ghost Ca ca ca ca ca Caverns is llllleeeeft… Mo-o-omm Mom Mom Mom!
MOM. Sweetheart, I I I I I think sh sh she may be—
DAD. It's OKa-a-a-y. Cccc calm down and pppppppput on tttttttthose ssssssssseat belts… BBBBBBBBBBBuckle up back there and look fff for a sign that sssays—

(A PARK RANGER jumps out.)

FAMILY. Sweetheart! DAD! LOOK OUT!

(The FAMILY dramatically lurches forward and back as DAD hits the breaks.)

DAD. I got it, I got it! I saw him. I saw him! It's OK, it's OK. I'll handle this now, let me do the talking here.

(The PARK RANGER walks deliberately to the car.)

PARK RANGER. Can I help you folks?

DAD. Sorry about that. We, uh, well, we're looking for the free parking for Ghost Caverns.

PARK RANGER. You're on the Ghost Caverns hiking trail, sir. What you want to do is turn around, go back about a mile, make your first left onto the road, and turn in by a big three-dimensional billboard…about the size of a battleship. Or, since you're here, you could park over there in the RV park and walk up the trail to the caverns.

MOM. And how far is that?

PARK RANGER. Maybe half a mile or so. It's a straight shot. You folks take care.

MOM. Thank you.

DAD. Well, gang, there's a hiking trail. What do you say—

SIS.	DON.
No! No! DAD! Please!	No, Dad, let's just drive back.

(Everyone piles out of the car.)

DAD. OK, OK. I say we put this to a family vote. Stay in the car and drive all the way back—

(The KIDS raise their hands and drop heads. MOM pulls their hands down. DAD has his back to the KIDS.)

DAD *(cont'd)*. Or take the Ghost Caverns trail, stretch the legs, take in some nature. And let's remember who got you here.

(MOM raises the KIDS' hands. DAD turns.)

DAD *(cont'd).* Now that's the Browning spirit. Let's head on out!

(They head out.)

SIS. Mom, this doesn't look like a trail.

MOM. Sweetheart, it's all right.

DAD. Follow me, gang. This way. One two, one two, hep hep hep hep...

SIS. Mom, why can't we drive?

MOM. Follow your father, sweetheart.

(They exit but are still heard on the next lines. DON lags behind, not exiting, setting up his next transition.)

DAD. Not to worry, your father was an Eagle Scout... AHHHHHHHHHHHHHH!

SIS. Holy crap, Dad fell!

MOM. Language, sweetheart, language!

(DON transitions. Looking at brochure.)

DON. Ghost Caverns, yeah, wow, one bat, no witches, and stalagmites the size of little tiny party hats...What a bust. But I have to say stops like those made our trips, well, better.

(DON enters diner. SFX: Door close with bell. DON sits.)

DON *(cont'd).* Wait a minute that's it! *(Beat.)* I could take you to the Dells! I've never been, you've never been, you might like it. Yeah, I know, bunch of over-priced shenanigans.

(WAYNE enters, a stoic, deadpan server with a mullet and a coffeepot. He stands next to DON, overly still, almost looming. DON studies the menu and becomes aware of WAYNE's presence.)

DON *(cont'd)*. Oh hi there, uhh, my car's getting fixed and they told me I could get a bite to eat here. So are you still serving?
WAYNE *(ominously still)*. Coffee, sir?
DON. Sure.
WAYNE. Jessie will be your server.
DON. Thank you.

(JESSIE enters.)

JESSIE. Boo!
WAYNE. That's her. *(Exits.)*
JESSIE. Hi, welcome to Gabby's, my name is Jessie, although most people think I'm Gabby, too. *(DON is too tired and agitated to respond.)* As in Gabby Jessie, not THE Gabby, although she's never here and that's not my problem. You're not too gabby at all. You look like you've had a tough day, Mr. Tuckered Out. You know what I'm calling you, Mr. Tuckered Out? I'm calling you Mr. Down in the Dumps, Mr. Tuckered Out. But my name's Jessie and you're in good hands. Now, is there anything else? Extra sugar? Sweet'n Low, cream, a clean spoon? Ha, I was fooling. Just fooling. That's what I do, I'm a fooler. We have the cleanest kitchen

this side of the Mississippi. See, Jessie's funny. She's a
fooler and she's funny. C'mon, that was funny and I
know it was funny. People tell me all the time, Jessie,
take that one on the road, but I'd rather be here for you.
So, you catch your breath, Mr. Slouchyface. Let me
know what you want, and Jessie'll get it for you, OK?
OK? OK? OK?

DON. OK.

JESSIE. OK. You just let me know now and Jessie will get
it for you because that's what I do. *(Exits.)*

DON *(pause)*. How about let Wayne be my server? Can I
let you know that?

(WAYNE approaches DON's table with coffee.)

WAYNE *(flat)*. More coffee, sir?

DON. No, thank you, Wayne.

WAYNE. They're still checking on your car.

DON. You're a man of few words, Wayne. I like that.

WAYNE. Jessie will still be your server.

(JESSIE reenters.)

JESSIE. OK, now what can I get for my Mr. Smiley here?
I highly recommend our meatloaf cutlet. It's got
Wayne's three-part gravy. That's one part gravy, two
parts Wayne—ha! Joke.

WAYNE. Ha, Jessie's funny. *(Walks away.)*

JESSIE. Thanks, Wayne. He's sweet... It's real good, but
if you're looking for something light, I'd go with the
hog butcher's omelette. Ham, bacon, sausage, three

kinds of cheese, and Egg Beaters...that's what keeps it light. So what's it gonna be?

DON. I just want a plain burger, no pickle, no onions and some ketchup.

JESSIE. That's it?

DON. That's it.

JESSIE *(shouting)*. Wayne! Kill it, grill it and give it to him simple. *(To DON.)* What do we have here? *(Picks up brochures.)* What's this? "Wax the day away at Candle Gardens"? Now that sounds fun. Though I'll tell ya, last Christmas my sister bought me a scented rabbit candle and I told her I thought she could find a better way to say Merry Christmas than a lilac bunny with a wick in his butt. Rude maybe, but that's Jessie, honest to a fault. I mean, heck, my cousin Becky, who's not even a real cousin, got me some fakey pearl earrings for my birthday. Fakey pearl is my birthstone. Well, not fakey, but pearl. But you see where I'm going with this, I'm just saying a couple of fakey pearl earrings mean a heckuva lot more than a lilac bunny with a wick in his butt. I mean if you're gonna do something, make it mean something, 'cause it's family, don't ya think?

(SFX: Diner daydream music. A special on DON as JESSIE fades but continues gesturing in silent conversation. DAD enters and stands off to the side of the stage, listening to DON.)

DON. Maybe I should just leave you here. Maybe you'd like Jessie? Or maybe this is it. Maybe this is where I say I'm sorry, Dad. I'm sorry Grandma's house is a grocery store. I'm sorry. Sorry for missing dinner and sorry for lying about the car. I'm sorry the Cougars never won a state title. I'm sorry we didn't talk more. I'm sorry that I'm in a diner in the middle of Iowa saying I'm sorry. I'm sorry that it snows in Boston, and flights get canceled and I'm sorry *(long pause)*,

(SFX: Sorry music.)

DON *(cont'd)*. I'm sorry that I missed your funeral. Maybe that's the whole story right there. "Selfish, guilty, stupid son misses flight, misses funeral, drives endlessly around Iowa, ends up with Jessie and Wayne." Sorry, Dad, I tried.

(Music ends. Lights change. DAD exits.)

DON *(cont'd)*. Cancel my order.
JESSIE. It'll be out in a minute.
DON. Look, I'm just going home. Cancel it.
JESSIE. Home? Where ya from, Mr. Cancel?
DON. Boston.
JESSIE. Boston!
DON. No, I mean—
JESSIE. Boston. Oh my goodness, we've got a dead man driving if you try to drive all the way to Boston tonight.
DON. No...
JESSIE. Now you listen to me, Mr. Chalk Outline on the Side of the Road, you will not make it around the parking lot, let alone all the way to—
DON. Winterset! I'm going to Winterset. I'm just driving to my hometown, Winterset, Iowa. Just cancel the burger.

JESSIE *(completely excited)*. Winterset? That's Home of the Duke.

DON. Yes, I know, but—

JESSIE. He's my favorite. I musta seen *Rio Bravo* and *The Green Berets* I bet a hundred times. Jessie's right, isn't she, that's home of the Duke. I know I'm right I just know it. Say it with me, Mr. Slouchyface. Winterset is—

DON *(yelling)*. YES! YES! Winterset, Winterset is home of the Duke! *(Pause.)*

(WAYNE rushes in and stares. DON takes a moment.)

DON *(cont'd)*. I'm sorry, really, I'm sorry. I needed you to stop talking.

JESSIE. Look, Mr. Angry, I was just trying to help, but I don't care what you do after this display of rudeness. So why don't you take your brochures and go talk to yourself in Rock Country and Wax Candle Park, or just go be rude rude rudey to yourself in the center of the United States in Leba—whatever Kansas for all I care. *(Slaps the brochures down on the table like cards and walks away.)*

DON *(pause)*. What did you say? *(DON picks up one of the brochures.)*

JESSIE *(raises palm)*. Eh—I'm not talking, remember? You may leave now, or maintain Wayne as your server, but *we* are through. *(JESSIE exits.)*

(SFX: Stand in the center music. DAD enters.)

DON & DAD. The center? "Come stand in the center of your country."

(SFX: Car pass. Lights change. DAD is craning his head at a billboard they just drove by.)

DAD. "Come stand in the center of your"—what? Did you see that?

MOM. What was that, honey?

DAD. That billboard back there. Said something about the center of the country or something.

(SFX: Car pass.)

DAD *(cont'd)*. Well, there it is, kids, it's official. We are now leaving Hannibal. Wave goodbye. Wave goodbye, kids.

DON. Give it to me.

SIS. I don't have it. Ouch!

MOM. Settle down back there—we have a long drive ahead of us here and I'm already nearing the end of my patience.

DAD. Maybe it's time to do our review. Whattya say? "I had a great time when I went to…" *(No response.)* "I had a great time when I went to…"

SIS. I'm tired.

DAD. OK, OK, maybe later.

DON. Mom, she took my arrowhead, I know it.

SIS. I did not take his stupid arrowhead.

MOM & DAD. Hey!

MOM. What did we say about that word?

DON. Yes she did. Tell her to give it back.

SIS. I don't have it.

MOM. OK, now, why don't you both just take a break, grab those books and do a little reading?

DON & SIS. But, Mom—
DAD. Do what your mother says.
SIS. Mom, I'm sick of stupid, stupid, stupid Mark Twain.
DAD. Hey!

(KIDS start fighting. MOM rises and walks around the back of the car, grabbing both KIDS by the arm.)

MOM. OK, OK, OK, that's it! That is it! I have had it with both of you! I am sick of both of you, do you hear me? All of your whining and complaining. You know, we don't have to come on these vacations. I should have told your father not to stop at Ghost Caverns because you sure don't deserve it. What you deserve is a good old-fashioned spanking. But instead we are going to sit back here and read until we are through with this book. And if you don't pretend to enjoy every second of it we will read it again. Do I make myself clear? *(The KIDS nod in shame. MOM comes around and settles between them. To SIS.)* You start here. *(To DON.)* And you follow along, because you're reading next.
SIS. The Celebrated Jumping Frog of Cala—Cala— Cala—
DAD. Calaveras. You picked a good one, sweetpea. That Celebrated Frog of Calaveras County.

(SFX: Hannibal music enters, gently underneath.)

SIS. "There was a gambling fellow by the name of Jim Smiley and if there was a dog fight, he'd bet on it; if there was a cat fight, he'd bet on it; if there was a chicken fight, he'd bet on it; if he even seen a straddle bug start to go anywhere, he would bet you how long it would take him to get wherever he was going—" *(Out of book.)* Mom, this guy has a problem.

MOM. Just keep reading.

DON. Dad, what's a straddle bug?

DAD. That's your basic beetle, son.

SIS. "But in truth they say Mr. Smiley was a lucky, lucky man."

(SFX: Car pass.)

DAD. Hey, there it is again. *(Reads-squints.)* "Come stand in the center of your country." Huh. I'm sorry, sounding good back there. Keep reading, go on.

MOM. OK, Don, start here.

DON *(as if reading)*. Even with the never-ending search for cheap hotels with toxic pools, getting lost, and trapped inside a station wagon that could double for a crock pot, and the tireless fixation on the least interesting parts of history, in spite of it all, Mom sitting on the hump, and watching you listen to us read, made it, I have to say, better.

DAD *(laughing)*. I like what I'm hearing back there. What'd I tell ya? It's a classic, an absolute classic.

DON. And you laughing. God, to hear you laugh.

DAD. I like what I'm hearing. You betcha. You have to admit, that is one lucky frog. One lucky, lucky frog.

(SFX: Car pass.)

DAD *(cont'd)*. Hey, there it is again. *(Pointing.)* "Come stand in the center."

(FAMILY exits on the next lines.)

MOM. OK, sweetie, right here.

SIS *(fading down and out)*. "And he used to win money on
that horse, for all she was so slow…"

*(Lights change. DON transitions from back seat to
diner. DON is focused on the brochure as WAYNE reenters.)*

DON. Come stand in the center of your country. Come
stand in the center of your country.

WAYNE *(shrugs)*. Fred called. Your car's fixed.

DON. NO! You're kidding! Wow, that's perfect. That is
great, Wayne, you have no idea! Wayne, I bet you get
feelings, don't you? I mean you believe in karma, don't
ya? Look at you, sure you do, because here's the deal,
Wayne. My dad passed away three year ago and, well,
we got busy and left him in the basement, and now he's
out in the car… *(WAYNE's confused.)* I mean his ashes,
Wayne, his ashes, and until just a moment ago I was
pretty unsure as to what to do with 'em but now I have
this. *(Waving brochure.)* So do me a favor and give this
to Jessie and tell her I'm sorry. *(Hands WAYNE money.)*
Wayne, you ever been to the Dells? Yeah well, me neither, so take some for yourself and go to the Dells, will
ya do that for me, Wayne? I promise you won't regret it.
But I've got to get going, Wayne, and I'm going to be
OK, even if I end up driving all night I'll be OK, because, Wayne, *(pause)* I think I might be on some kind
of damn adventure. I can feel it. *(Exiting.)* OK? Tell
Jessie I'm sorry— OOOKKKAYYYY?

(WAYNE follows DON and calls out.)

WAYNE. Wait, who are the Dells? And where can I find them? *(WAYNE exits.)*

(SFX: Phone rings. Phone call music in softly. OLDER MOM walks out on one side, OLDER SIS on the other. Each deliver their part of a phone conversation with DON.)

OLDER MOM. Kansas? Kansas? What in heaven's name are you doing all the way out in Kansas?

OLDER SIS. Really? A grocery store?

OLDER MOM. Please don't drive all night like your father did.

OLDER SIS. So you lied to Mom. I can't believe you lied to Mom.

OLDER MOM. I swear I could never get that man to pull over and—

OLDER SIS. And you lied to me! Well, I can believe you lied to me, but...

OLDER MOM. He'd drive all night and scare me half to death.

OLDER SIS. I can't believe you missed dinner and stuck me with Uncle Phil.

OLDER MOM. Well, I hope to God you will pull over if you're tired.

OLDER SIS. Well, I hope to God your car breaks down again and you have to walk home.

OLDER MOM. I trust you, sweetheart. Just get home safe and sound.

OLDER SIS. You're a liar and I think you're crazy.

OLDER MOM. OK then, just tell me all about it when you
    get home.
OLDER SIS. Yeah, I remember that night, sure. I don't
    think you'll find it, but I remember it.
OLDER MOM. Just get home safe.
OLDER SIS. Good luck, big brother.
OLDER MOM. I love you.
OLDER SIS. I love you.

*(They exit. Lights fade and bright morning light comes
up on DON. He is lost, tired and looking at the traveler's guide. BOB, a farmer in overalls, enters and
stares a couple beats, looking at DON.)*

BOB *(calling out)*. Morning, stranger. You look a little
    lost.
DON. Huh? Oh yeah, I'm afraid you're right. I just don't
    see how.
BOB. Where you heading?
DON. Well, I thought there, *(pointing to map)* which I
    thought was around here.
BOB. Yeah? You wanted to come to my hog farm?
DON. Well, no, maybe, yes, near it at least, I think.
    (Pointing to road.) Now this is Route 93?
BOB. Yep.
DON. And I'm in Kansas?
BOB. Yep.
DON. OK, OK, then, well, that's the problem. I made it to
    Lebanon, and I'm trying to find this spot about forty
    miles outside—
BOB. Well, I'll be.
DON. Supposedly, it's the center—

DON & BOB. Of the United States.

DON. Yes, you know it?

BOB. Well, I'll be. I'll be. Hold on, partner. Hey, Jude, Judy, we got ourselves a visitor.

DON. It's here?

BOB. You're closer than you know.

(JUDY enters.)

DON. So it's here? *(Confused.)* Right here?

BOB. Well, yes—

JUDY. And no.

DON. I'm sorry?

BOB. We will definitely show you where you want to go, but first off, this is my wife, Judy—

DON. Hi, Judy, Don Browning. Nice to meet you.

JUDY. Hi, Don, nice to meet you, too.

BOB. And I'm Bob Peneplain and we'd sure like to welcome you to Peneplains Hog Farm. *(BOB gives DON his right arm for a handshake; BOB's hand is missing.)*

DON. Thanks, Bob. At least it looks like I'm talking to the right guy.

BOB. Yep, yep, yep, yep. *(Holding up his stump.)* Not much there. It got clipped off by the baler. Didn't hurt one bit. I can't say I did much with it anyway.

JUDY. Oh, Bob.

BOB. I used to shake with the left hand, but it never did feel natural... Go ahead give it a run. *(Offers DON his left hand. They shake.)* See what I mean? It's like a man wearing two right shoes and walking backwards in a stiff breeze. It's just not natural.

JUDY. Now, Bob.

DON. No, I see what you mean…

BOB. You ever seen a baler?

BOB.	JUDY.
Because, boy when they come at you, let me tell you—	Bob, Bob, but not so much right now.

BOB. She's right, she's right. OK, Jude, I'll go get the camera. *(BOB exits.)*

JUDY. Boy, it sure has been a while since anyone's come looking for the center. Where you from, Don?

DON. Boston.

JUDY. Boston, well, well. Sorry, you'll have to excuse Bob. He gets pretty excited whenever we get a visitor.

DON. So it is here?

JUDY. Well, yes and no.

DON. I'm sorry?

JUDY. Don, you see, back in 1955 a team of what we figure were pretty bored and lonely geographers set out to find the exact center of the United States, and they decided that almost where we are right now was the center.

DON. So this is it?

JUDY. Actually, look out there, a little past the hog tins and over to the right…in that field is a white pole—

(BOB enters.)

BOB. A very rusty white pole.

JUDY. And on that pole is a sign.

BOB. She won't let me paint it.

JUDY. The sign says, "The center—you are here."

(BOB snaps a Polaroid of DON and JUDY.)

BOB.	JUDE.
Hey, Jude, take a look.	Bob, Bob.
You look good.	BOB! Not so much right now.

BOB. She's right, she's right.

JUDY. Now, for the longest time that pole was considered the dead bone center of our country.

BOB. People came from miles around.

JUDY. From everywhere you could imagine. It was just a happy, good time.

BOB. That is—

JUDY. That is until one of our so-called kindly neighbors decided to put up their own version of the center pole.

BOB. Sons of bastards. Dirty sons of bastards. They all said they were the center.

JUDY. Bob, Bob, Bob…

BOB. I'm sorry, Judy, but how can there be more than one center? The center is the center and we were it. I'm sorry, Jude, but it's true.

JUDY *(sharply)*. Bob!

BOB. She's right, she's right…

JUDY. Well, Bob's upset here because as you may or may not imagine there was simply not enough interest to support two geographical centers of our country. And in time, well, it all just went away.

BOB *(under breath)*. Sons o' bastards. Dirty sons o'—

JUDY. Now the center's officially been closed twenty-two years now—

BOB. —and two months—

JUDY. But once in a rare while a curious soul like yourself
    comes wandering by—

BOB. You're number sixty-two, Don.

JUDY *(to BOB)*. Is that right? Bob likes to keep track.

BOB. Jude? *(Holding the picture and a pen.)*

JUDY. Bob wants you to sign that picture there, and give it
    a date, if that's OK.

DON. Sure.

JUDY. But what we'd truly like is to hear your story. The
    story about what on God's green earth brought someone
    all the way from Boston clear out here to the center.

DON. Wow. Well, Judy, it was this beaten-up traveler's
    guide that got me out here this far, but to be honest, it's
    a story about pulling over, and taking one week a year...
    But mostly it's a story about my dad.

*(SFX: Flashback music. Lights change. The following
lines are all delivered on top of one another. The FAM-
ILY uses them to reenter the car. They are picking back
up in the opening scene, reenacting it all the same way.)*

DAD.	MOM.
Who's not sleeping?	We need a mile marker.
Who's not sleeping?	We need a mile marker.

DON.	SIS.
Mo-o-o-o-o-o-o-om!	Mom, it's not fair,
Mo-o-o-o-o-o-o-om!	it's not fair.
Mo-o-o-o-o-o-o-om!	it's not fair!

(Lights up.)

SIS. If it's a promise and a vote, then I promise I'm never voting again!

DAD. OK, that's it, that is it. That is it! I am pulling over!

(SFX: Pull over.)

MOM *(pause, whispering)*. I still need a mile marker.

DAD. Everyone, we are not lost. We've just gotten a little off track.

SIS. Mom!

DON.   MOM.
Shh!   Shh!

MOM *(to DAD with great concern)*. Honey?

DAD. OK, here's the deal.

(SFX: Car pass.)

DAD *(cont'd)*. We all know Hannibal was a little disappointing. And after Ghost Caverns turned out to be less than advertised, well, I just couldn't stop thinking about those billboards I kept seeing about the center. I couldn't stop thinking about our family in the middle of the United States and what a great picture that would be for our mantel, and for Grandma. So when I got to the sign that said, "Last chance to visit the center—this exit," I took it.

SIS. What?

MOM. Shh!

DAD. And let me say I thought we'd be there by now, take the picture and be on our way. Now I admit we're a little lost, but we are close, I can feel it. And I just keep seeing that picture of all of us…

SIS. But, Dad…

DAD. Now, sweetheart, I know I promised we'd go to Grandma's, and we will, but it's never too late to make a trip a little more special. *(KIDS react.)* I guess it's only fair to put this to a vote. *(KIDS' heads fall.)* So… all in favor of turning around…

(DON and SIS raise their hands. After a beat, so does MOM. DAD does not see it.)

DAD *(cont'd).* Very good. And now all in favor of going—

(MOM gently puts her hand on DAD's arm, calling attention to her vote. DAD takes a beat.)

DAD *(cont'd).* All right. OK. Then that's what we'll do. That's what we'll do.

(SFX: Dad turns around music. DAD turns around. The FAMILY drives in silence for a while as the music swells. Lights begin to fade and the FAMILY rises. NOTE: DO NOT RUSH THIS MOMENT. After enough time has passed, the FAMILY stands and move their car boxes to the side of the stage, clearing the stage. Several options for car clearing can be used.

SFX: Outdoor noise. BOB and JUDY reenter, meeting DON in the center of the stage. JUDY hands DON the traveler's guide.)

BOB. That's quite a story there, Don. Quite a story.

JUDY. Yep, that's a real nice thing you're doing there.

BOB. Sure is, sure is.

JUDY. Ya know, Don, Bob and I like to think we know people when we meet 'em. I have to say that you did real good when you shook the stump.

BOB. You sure did.

JUDY. Some people flinch a bit.

BOB. They sure do.

JUDY. But not you.

BOB. Sure didn't.

JUDY. And that shows character.

BOB. Sure does.

JUDY. Some real character.

BOB. Sure does.

JUDY. So, Don, we'd be honored to have your father grace our center pole. Now understand, I don't walk out there anymore. It's too upsetting. But Bob will walk you out. You OK with that, Bob?

BOB. Sure am, Jude.

JUDY. Maybe I'll see you boys later. Nice to meet you, Don.

DON. Nice to meet you, too, Judy.

(BOB and DON start walking. BOB stops DON.)

BOB. Be careful, friend. Watch your step or you might be taking a little of Peneplains Farm home with ya.

(DAD enters with center pole, taking it to its designated spot. He remains on stage.)

DON. Will do, Bob.

BOB. You get used to it.

DON *(walks a little)*. So was this your dad's farm?

BOB. No, no. My father was a biologist of sorts. One of the first to really start work on hybrid corn seed.

DON. No kidding.

BOB. See how that corn is out there? All nice and straight and even? My dad did that. It's called the Sturdy Stalk Effect. And that's what they call it, Sturdy Stalk.

DON. Really?

BOB. Yep. Whenever I look out over a field of corn all nice and even I think of him. That was his contribution to this life. Sturdy Stalk. And me. *(Beat.)* Well, I'll let ya be. *(BOB turns. DON stops him.)*

DON. Hey, Bob—thanks.

(DON offers BOB his hand and shakes the stump. BOB walks away. DON gathers himself at the center pole.)

DON *(cont'd)*. Well, you would think standing in the center of the country might inspire even an average writer. But all I can think to say, Dad, is, we made it, it's a hog farm, it's beautiful, and, *(beat)* man, does it stink.

(SFX: Piano music.)

DON *(con't., pause)*. I never told you that whenever I sit down to write, the first word that goes through my head is "unpredictable," Browning's are unpredictable. "Fascinating," I try to avoid, but unpredictable helps, and now that I have the chance I'd like say *(beat)* getting here has been some kind of damned adventure.

(NOTE: Be careful not to play DON's final moments with DAD sad but more quietly exhilarated and upbeat.

Lights change to nighttime. DON moves to his corner as if to take one last look at the field and think about his father. MOM, DAD and SIS enter standing in the corners of the stage in soft pools of light, near their boxes. They all act as if they are still in the car, driving.)

SIS *(yawning)*. Are we there yet?

MOM. Almost home, almost home. *(To DAD.)* Maybe next year we'll get back there.

DAD. Oh, that's fine, that's fine. I just hope the kids had fun.

MOM. Oh, you know they did, you know they did.

DAD. OK, everybody up and out. Up and out.

SIS. Mom?

DAD. Looks like we're home.

MOM. Look around, make sure you're not forgetting anything.

DAD. C'mon, shake it out. Shake it out.

MOM. OK, no empty hands. Everyone grab something.

SIS. Mom, where's my book?

MOM. It's in my bag, sweetheart, it's in my bag.

(SFX: End theme music. MOM turns to DAD, who is lagging behind by the "car" at center stage.)

MOM *(cont'd)*. Honey?

DAD. Just getting the mileage, dear.

MOM. OK.

(MOM and SIS walk offstage. DAD and DON are standing center stage alone, looking out.)

DAD. Quite a trip, eh, big guy?

DON. Yes, sir.

DAD. You betcha, quite a trip…

(DON's and DAD's movements mirror each other as DAD moves to the house, and DON is moving away from the pole to the car. DON stops and then DAD stops also. DON looks down at the old traveler's guide, he smiles, turns and sets it next to the pole and the urn.)

DON. You betcha.

(He turns one final time, and they look out over the cornfield together and then DON and DAD exit. Lights fade. Music plays out.)

THE END

(SFX: Walkout music: "I've Been Iowhere.")

PRODUCTION NOTES

Leaving Iowa is a memory play that weaves together past and present. In the premiere production at the Purple Rose Theatre, director Tony Caselli chose to have the dad present on stage, watching and listening to Don as he remembers moments from his youth and contemplates his current dilemma. Thankfully, Dad did not appear as a ghost, but more as a reassuring presence that represents the influence our parents have inside all of us, even when they are gone. This choice also made for quick, smooth transitions and kept this sentimental comedy squarely where it needed to be—in the mind of Don and in the heart of a dad that tried too hard. Also, realize that Don's memories are not reality but rather an exaggeration of his pain and love of these family road trips. Be bold in both the emotion and the silliness.

Some tangible suggestions:

1. Don't play the movement in the car literally. Have the kids stand up, allow Mom and Dad to jump up outside the car to discipline the children; whatever works for the moment. Playing the confines of an actual car is boring and comically restrictive.

2. Make sure the kids in the back seat sit high enough above Mom and Dad so we can see their reactions.

3. We encourage a simple choice when considering the car itself, such as the use of four stools or wooden boxes. The boxes have proven to be sturdier, allowing for stronger physical play, but both have been successful.

4. A minimalist approach to the set seems to serve the play best, highlighting character over time-consuming set changes, with actors themselves moving set pieces on, off and around the stage as they perform.

5. Once the urn is established, feel free to have Don stick it behind the seat until he needs it. The urn is a necessary setup device but a visual downer. Besides, Dad's on-stage presence listening to his son is more important and obviously more compelling than the urn.

6. Some productions of the play have made use of a cap for Don to help indicate switching from past to present.

7. Don't be consumed with how old or young Don and Sis might be. Play the exuberance, playfulness and typical give and go that a young angst-filled brother and sister share. The script has Don as the little brother, but you may cast an older Don if you choose and use "big brother" on lines where he is referred to as "little brother."

8. Note on Don's narration: When Don is speaking out loud as adult Don, do everything you can to avoid having him sound like a typical narrator. He should always be in the moment, trying to figure out what is the next best move. Don's talking out loud to himself gives us the feeling of being in Don's head instead of being lead down a path. However, when Don is a child, direct address feels natural and is the best and most humorous approach. Still, you must always keep him in the scene, never feeling the need to step out and stop the action in order to speak.

SOUND DESIGN CD NOTES

The Sound Design CD Set is required for performance.

The set contains original background and incidental music (such as Driving music, Phone Call music), transition SFX (such as a car passing), and complimentary SFX (car starting, picture sound).

Pre-Show and Intermission Music: Original songs by Sons of the Never Wrong.

The use of specific sounds and an original musical score fill a critical and invaluable role in bringing this travel play to life and helping pull Don and the story fluidly and effortlessly from scene to scene. The music and sound almost serve as a second narrator; a simple car passing adds information in many ways. There are more than 50 sound cues used in many instances, all crafted and refined from the early productions. They are the glue that holds the story together.

SET

Some productions have incorporated elaborate set elements, others have been intentionally sparse. The show has been produced on both proscenium and thrust stages; it adapts well to either.

These are some of the more essential pieces that need to be considered:

ACT I

• CAR: The most versatile car has been made of wood boxes, two for the front seat (approx 16" square) and a back seat that is a bench (36" high, 24" deep, 48" wide). Stools have also been used for all four of the seats. The most critical aspect is to make sure the back seat is significantly higher than the front seat to make the children visible to the audience. Another important element is storage for small props for all characters, e.g., the traveler's guide, kids' books, View-Master, etc. This can be done easily with side pockets attached to the seats. Lastly, this entire design must be mobile to be easily struck for final scene.

• SILO: It's been everything from a ladder on a pole to a visual-only silo to a climbable silo.

• FENCE: This has been a small piece of picket fence held by the actors (i.e. Grandma and Grandpa), or some have chosen to make it an actual picket fence that is part of the set (but still carried off with Grandma and Grandpa).

• GROCERY CART: An actual grocery cart; can be the smaller drugstore size.

• PHONE NOOK: For Mom; used four times—quick on and off. Phone itself can be merely implied (offstage focus) but not pantomimed. (Note: Don's cell phone should be "real.")

• BAR SCENE: Several options: Jack and Don have stood behind the back seat of the car with beers in hand, or they've used a little bar table that flips out. Some people have chosen to make the bar in Act I the same as the diner table in Act II.

ACT II

• HOTEL DESK (FOR CLERK): Can be a flip-down desk, a roll-out desk, or something else. Whatever it is, a brochure rack is a welcome touch versus the brochures lying on the counter.

• DINER: Again, the back seat has been used, or whatever bar scene set items that are used. NOTE: Don needs to be facing out to audience.

• CENTER POLE: The pole must have a sign on it: "The Center – You Are Here." Dad brings the pole out (as Bob and Don walk to the Center) and places it approximately center stage, depending on other staging choices. NOTE: car must be struck.

PROP LIST

Mark Twain storybooks (4)	Preset in pockets of car. (You will ultimately need 6 books total; extra books in the pockets of the car are recommended to avoid tracking problems.)
Steering wheel	Dad enters with it.
Traveler's guide	Starts off with Mom. Used throughout show.
Offstage crash box	Used twice in this scene: Once at the top of the scene (single crash) then again when Sis is looking for urn.
Urn in a box with dust	Sis enters with it. The urn alone will be used throughout show.
Baby powder for dust on urn	A thin coat should be sprinkled on top of it to be blown off.
Stenographer's notepad with pen	Should be preset in Don's pocket.
One arrowhead on a string	Sis gives it to Don.
Small sack lunch	Mom brings in from offstage and gives to Don.
Jacket (not worn)	Mom brings in from offstage and gives to Don.
Don's baseball cap	Mom brings in from offstage and gives to Don.
Vintage View-Master w/ slides	Sis enters with it.
Hand towel	Mom comes out with it.
Mark Twain storybooks (2)	Dad enters with them.
Mom's oversized handbag w/ multiple compartments	Mom enters with it.
Vintage magazine	In Mom's handbag.

Prop	Note
Cross-stitch for Mom in car	In Mom's handbag.
Notecard	Preset on Sis. Sis reads her speech off of it.
Nickel	Preset on Dad. Dad hands it to Sis.
String for cat's cradle	Don and Sis use it.
Bag of lollipops	Mom hands out two per show.
Plate w/ Rice Krispie treat the size of cement block	Grandma enters with it. Should be one giant Krispie treat. (Literally, cement block-sized.)
	Grandpa enters with it.
Gate	Pushed on from offstage.
Grocery cart	For Cart Guy.
Walkie-Talkie	Sis enters with it.
Mixing bowl and spoon	Preset in Don's pocket.
Cell phone (flip-not stylish)	Preset in Mom's bag. Does not need to work.
Vintage Polaroid camera w/ neck strap	Joe Hofingers brings it on.
Old can for a spittoon	Joe Hofingers brings it on.
Old hoe	Preset in Dad's pocket.
Arrowhead	Jack enters with them.
Beer bottles (2)	Amish Guy enters with it.
Amish quilt	Dad enters with it.
Local tour map	Civil War Guy enters with it.
Musket with boyonet	Museum Assistant comes in with it.
Notecard	Preset in Civil War Guy's pocket.
Tennis ball for bayonet tip	Mechanic enters with it.
Small mechanic's flashlight	

(continued next page)

Phone	For hotel.
Brochure rack	For hotel.
Key rack	For hotel.
Multiple keys	For hotel.
Brochures (a lot of them)	For hotel.
Counter bell	For Clerk.
Neck brace	For Clerk.
Cane or crutch	Drunk Lady enters with it.
Ice bucket w/ ice in it	Park Ranger enters with it.
Big flashlight	Preset in upstage box seat.
Caddy for ketchup/mustard, sugar, salt/pepper, etc.	Wayne enters with it.
Coffee cup and saucer	Wayne enters with it.
Coffee pot, liquid	Preset in upstage box seat.
Menus	Jessie enters with it.
Waitress pen and pad	Preset on Don. Don gives to Wayne.
A few dollar bills	Don enters with it. (You will need 2.)
Traveler's guide	Bob enters with it.
Polaroid camera (functioning – 1 photo)	One photo is taken per show.
A bulk of Polaroid film	Bob enters with it.
Sharpie	Dad enters with it.
Center Pole w/ sign ("You are here")	

NOTES

NOTES

NOTES

NOTES